HOPES

AND

FEARS

One Couple's Fertility Challenges

DANNY COHEN

Contents

Contents

Contents

Contents

Preface

I have chosen to share my personal diary about the struggles I have
had with infertility with you.

I hope this will help those who have been blessed and have never
struggled with the challenges of infertility understand those
who have struggled. I have done this simply because infertility
is extremely emotionally pressing, and someone who has never
experienced it may not be able to understand its difficulties.

At the time of publishing, we have been married three years, and
we are still not blessed with children. I personally wrote this diary
and tried to include the struggles and difficulties my wife, Etty,
has also had, but it is I writing it, and Etty's feelings may not be so
prevalent.

I am a *Frum Litvish* Jew (religious Orthodox) and will do my best to
explain our many laws and customs.

I also understand that infertility is somewhat of a taboo subject in
Jewish communities, but I think it is time people actually realized
what happens and what couples go through.

I really hope sharing my diary achieves what I set out to do.

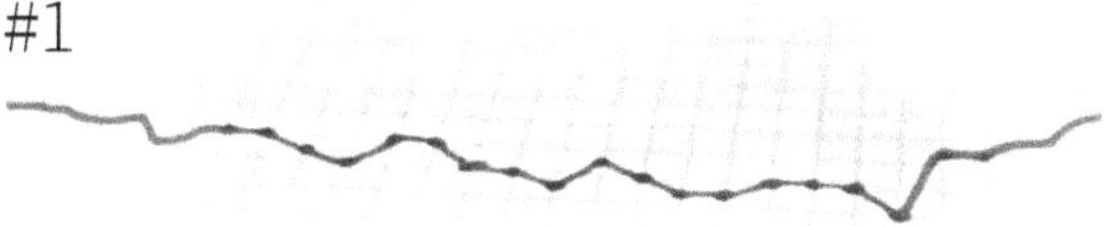

Six months married

Etty and I got married six months ago, and everything was perfect. Our wedding was beautiful, and the seven following *Sheva Brochas* (literally, seven blessings. It refers to the seven parties that take place for seven days after a Jewish wedding) were amazing. Four months ago, we moved to Israel and are planning on living here for two years, after which we plan on moving back abroad to our home town.

I am desperate to have children already and cannot wait to be a father. Every time Etty's period has been a day late, I run to the pharmacy and purchase a pregnancy test, hoping she is pregnant.

Today we celebrated our six-month anniversary, and while we reminisced about our first six months together, Etty told me that her *kallah* (bride) teacher had told her, "You should only start being worried about not becoming pregnant after six months of marriage." (It is customary for Orthodox Jews to have marital lessons with someone before getting married. They explain all the Jewish laws and customs regarding marriage, as well as give some marital advice and tips.) I think this is Etty's way of telling me she is worried that she is not yet pregnant. The truth is, I am also starting to wonder why Etty is not pregnant yet.

I keep on thinking that we are extremely young; Etty is only nineteen, and I'm twenty-one. But then I start thinking that in our Jewish community, it is not at all strange or unheard of. Most of my and Etty's friends and classmates are also married, and they are already pregnant.

Aliza, (my younger sister), gave birth after being married ten months, and I want a child too, so tomorrow we will go and see our family doctor.

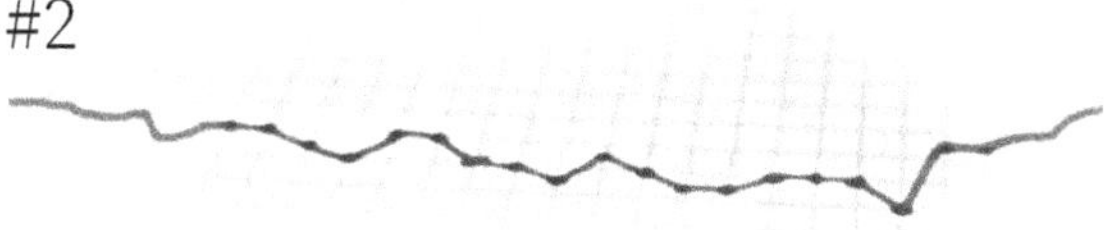

The doctor's appointment

I'm feeling relieved now, and my worries have gone away. The appointment today went very well. We saw a female doctor, and she asked Etty about her periods and said that everything was normal. She also gave us both referrals to have blood tests, which will double check and make sure all our hormones are balanced and everything is okay. Things are looking hopeful.

Blood test results

It took three days for the results to come, but finally this morning they were ready. We went back today to see the doctor, and she told us that everything was in order, and as far as she can tell, there is nothing wrong, and we have absolutely nothing to be worried about. She also explained the science behind becoming pregnant. Apparently, every month there is only a 20 percent chance of conceiving, so it's not really that strange that after being married six months, Etty is still not pregnant. She also gave us many blood test referrals, so that she can track Etty's ovulation, making sure she is actually ovulating and nothing is wrong. The next time Etty gets her period, she will need to go every morning and take a blood test; this is just to make sure Etty ovulates every month. Our feelings of worry have been put aside, and we both feel really relieved. I'm already thinking about Etty becoming pregnant in the next few months and can't wait to be a father.

#4

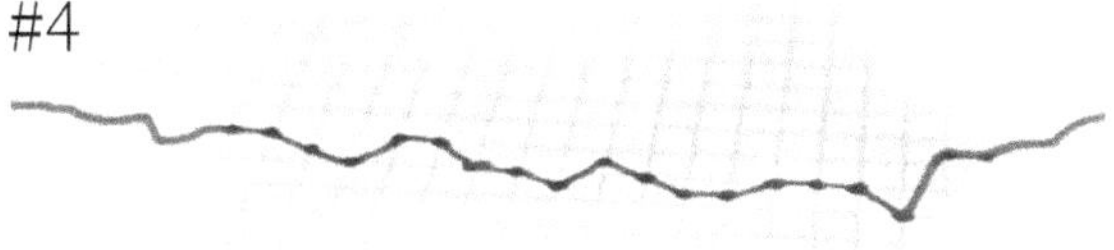

Etty ovulates

Two weeks ago, Etty got her period, so for the past two weeks, Etty has been getting up early every morning and taking a blood test. The nurse has even gotten to know her and is constantly asking her if she's okay, and every day she blesses her, telling her not to worry.

We went back to the doctor today, and she confirmed that Etty is ovulating like normal. So now we will wait, and hopefully Etty will become pregnant sooner rather than later.

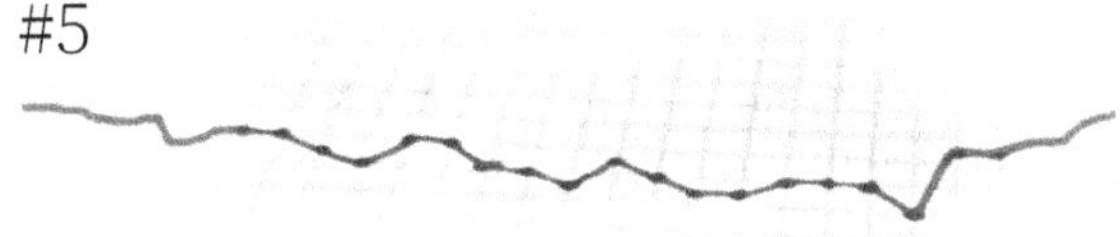

Why is Etty not pregnant?

Today we celebrated our first wedding anniversary. We went to eat out in a fancy restaurant, but the feeling of celebration is dampened with worry. The majority of Etty's friends who are married already have babies, and Etty feels out of place when she is around them. People have started looking at Etty's stomach when they meet her, before even looking at her face, just to see if she's pregnant. I don't understand this phenomenon. Why on earth is someone looking at someone else's stomach, determining if they are pregnant or not? Number one, who are they, and why is it their business? Number two, maybe they are newly pregnant and are not even showing yet. Number three, how do you think you would feel if someone looked at your stomach?

My parents are also starting to ask questions and wondering why we are not yet pregnant. I think my parents are the best parents in the world; they really love every single one of their children without any limit. But my mother is a really big worrier. She has asked me numerous times if everything is okay and if we have been to see any doctors yet. I keep on assuring her that we have been to a doctor and everything is just fine, and I keep on telling how some people take longer than others to become pregnant.

My in-laws have not mentioned anything to us about it. I think it is a bit strange, as my parents have asked us, but Etty keeps on telling me that it's not really their style to pry into other people's business.

Etty wanted me to speak to my rabbi today, who we both really respect, and ask him what he thinks about us not being pregnant yet, and what advice he has for us. So, I told him that we were really worried about Etty not being pregnant yet, and Etty is so upset about it that she doesn't like to leave our apartment unless she really has to. He told me that I need to understand where she is coming from. He explained how emotionally hard it is for a woman who is trying to become pregnant but hasn't conceived yet, and told me how Etty must be feeling, especially if she has friends who already have babies. He said she must be embarrassed to go out with them, and that I shouldn't force Etty to go anywhere she doesn't want to, although I should definitely talk to her, and try to get her to go out. He also reassured me that we are young and there is still plenty of time to become pregnant. He told me about the power of *davening* (praying). He said, "Many times, God just simply wants to hear us talking to Him and wants us to realize that He's in charge, instead of handing everything over to us on a silver platter." He also introduced me to an organization called Tahareinu that specializes in fertility and marital medical problems. I came away from the conversation feeling relieved and was happy to know that I had someone to talk to if I needed. I also called up Tahareinu and booked an appointment with Rabbi and Mrs. Melber, the heads of this wonderful organization.

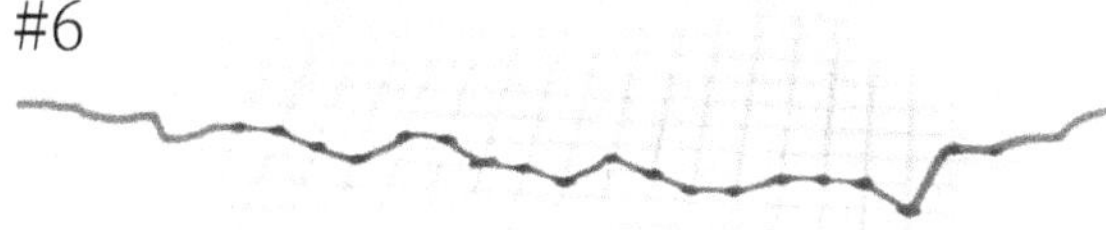

Tahareinu

The first thing I noticed when we came in was how everything is conducted in an extremely private manner. They are two doors leading to their office, with two separate rooms behind the doors, which then lead into a public corridor. This ensures that no one will see anyone else, and everyone's privacy is kept confidential. We arrived a bit early, and they were in the middle of a meeting with someone else, so the secretary told us to wait in one of the rooms till we are called. There were drinks, coffee, and some food for us to enjoy while we were waiting. We were both feeling really tense. Who knows what the Melbers would tell us? My mind was jumping to all crazy conclusions. What happens if they tell us we can never have children? What happens if they laugh at us and tell us we are both very young and we should stop being silly and come back in ten years' time?

Finally, their meeting was over. The people they were talking to left from the second door in their office to another empty room, and we entered the office from the first door.

We introduced ourselves and told them how we have been married for a year now and we're still not pregnant. We showed them the blood test results from six months ago and asked them what they thought. The first thing they did was assure us that we were not crazy for coming to them after being married for only a year. They explained how science has really advanced in the past few years, and how the doctors say if someone has been trying to conceive for a year without success, they should seek medical help. They told us that it doesn't matter what age we are; all that matters is how long we have been trying to conceive. So, this really helped calm me down, and I no longer felt stupid for coming to them.

They then opened up a new file for us and put in all our details. They asked us if we had Bituach Leumi (the Israeli national health insurance). I told them we did not have it yet, so they advised us to join it as soon as possible, as we would be needing it to see the fertility experts. They then told me that the next thing to do was a sperm test, and told me to discuss it with my rabbi, as there may be *Halachik* (Jewish law) ramifications. They also told us to do a few more blood tests that the family doctor had left out. They ended the meeting with them giving us their numbers and told us to message them if we ever have any questions. Rabbi Melber walked us out through the second door and assured me that within a year, Etty will be pregnant.

We are now feeling happy and relieved, confident that we are in good hands. The first thing I did after walking out of the building was make an appointment to sign up for Bituach Leumi and made a mental note to organize and get ready all the relevant documents needed. They told me that we needed papers from my *yeshivah* (Jewish college where we mainly study the Talmud), as well as our marriage certificate, Israeli entry and exit permits from the past year, and copies of our passports.

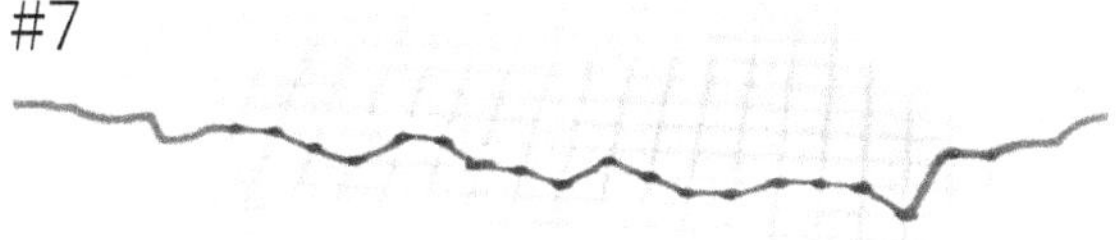

Halachik sperm clarification

I spoke to my rabbi today about taking a sperm test. He explained how in Jewish law, sperm tests are complicated and told me to be in touch with another organization called Machon Puah, which deals with all the Halachik requirements and difficulties of infertility. So, I called them up to book an appointment, but they told me there is no appointment needed, and I should just come during their open hours.

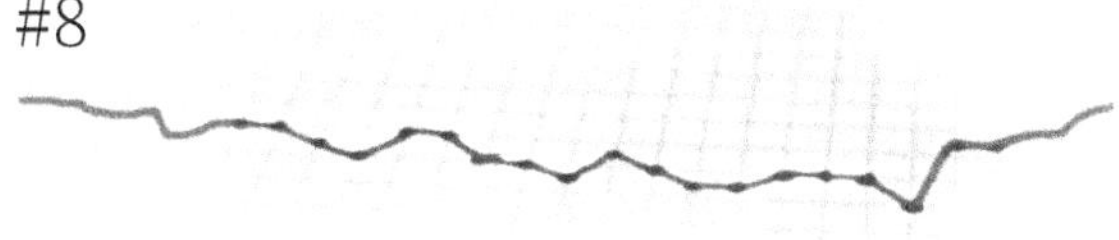

Machon Puah

This morning I went to Machon Puah and spoke to the rabbi there. He explained how in Judaism it is prohibited to spill seed without cause; we actually treat sperm as some sort of life form. He explained how scientifically, semen has thousands of sperm inside, so it is as though someone sheds actual blood and kills people, because every drop has the ability of creating thousands of generations of children. He then explained that using the sperm for evaluation or to help with infertility is not considered a waste; nevertheless they want to also make it possible for the sperm to be able to have the potential to impregnate there and then. So, he told me to use a condom, which must be purchased from them, as it has to be a sterilized and uncontaminated one. But before using it, I should make a small hole at the top of it using a sterilized needle; this way it is theoretically still possible for my sperm to impregnate Etty and is definitely not considered a waste.

After he finished explaining what I should do, I went upstairs to purchase it. Walking out of Machon Puah with the condom, I felt a whole wave of emotions being released. I felt embarrassed; in case I was seen by someone holding the condom, they would either think, *What on earth is a religious Jew doing with a condom?* or they would realize that I may have fertility problems and look at me with pity. Even though the condom was in a black bag and really impossible for anyone to see, my mind still wouldn't let these thoughts go away. I also felt extremely sad about not having a child yet and uncertain as to what the sperm results would tell me.

After getting home, I made an appointment at the sperm lab, and they told me that I need to be at the lab before eight thirty a.m., and the sperm cannot be more than an hour old. I started getting really worried. Will I be able to make it in time? What happens if we are just five minutes late? Will it be considered a waste of sperm?

I worked out that it will probably take me thirty-five minutes to get to the lab, which was in the center of Jerusalem, which means we would need to get up really early tomorrow. I have everything planned out; we will hopefully arrive at eight o'clock, because I don't want to miss the opportunity.

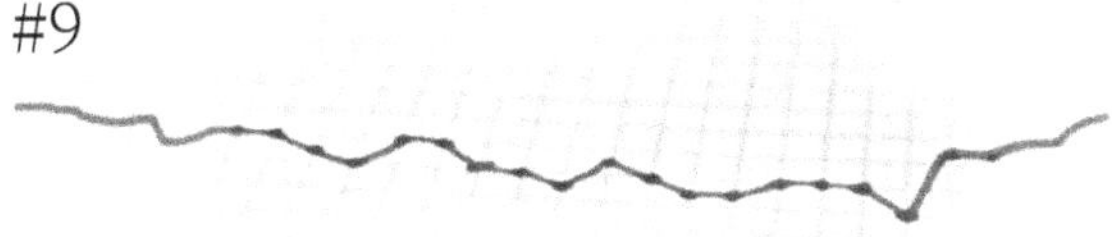

Sperm test

This morning, Etty and I were really pressured and realized that this couldn't fail; we couldn't arrive too late to the lab. So, we got up super early and left our apartment with time to spare. Thankfully, we arrived with ten minutes to spare. I gave them the sperm sample, paid for the test, and they told us to come back in an hour and a half and get the results.

The next hour and a half was really nerve wracking for us. What happens if the results come back really bad, and it's impossible for me to have children? We discussed how we knew people who were already married for ten years plus and didn't have children. We also knew people who were over sixty and had never had children. What happens if we are the same as them? We also spoke about how we didn't even know if sperm donations were allowed according to Jewish law, and even if it was allowed, would we really want to have a child that is partially not ours? My emotional world had been turned upside down, and Etty was really nervous too. I was pacing up and down, like I always do when I'm feeling stressed and nervous.

Finally, the ninety minutes were over; we came back to the lab with apprehension and asked for the test results. The lady handed them over and told us I had a perfect sperm count, and everything else was great as well. We were extremely relieved and really happy; my worst fear had vanished. I sent the results to Mrs. Melber, and she confirmed that everything was good.

All that was left to do was get Bituach Leumi, and then we would be able to see the fertility experts.

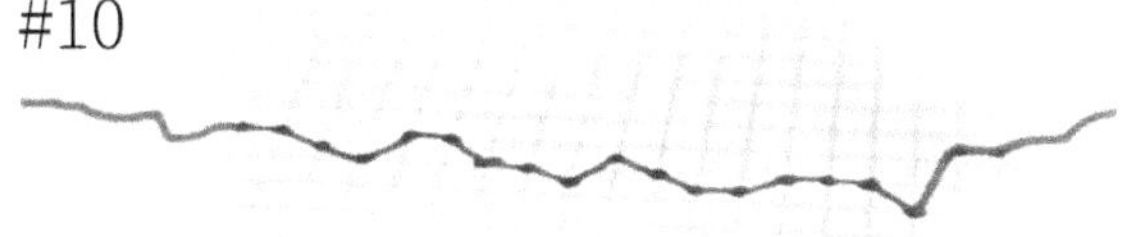

Bituach Leumi

Today, eventually after three months of waiting, the letter from Bituach Leumi arrived. Three months ago, we went to the Bituach Leumi office with all the relevant documents. They had told us everything was in order, and we should receive the confirmation letters in the mail. I have been checking the mailbox every single day waiting for that letter, and finally the letter has arrived. I went to the post office and gave them the letter, paying whatever needed to be paid. They linked our new Bituach Leumi account to our existing Meuhedet (medical insurance company) account, confirming that everything has been arranged, and we should get our new Meuhedet card in the mail soon. I then went to the Meuhedet office to confirm that everything had been done correctly, and they told me everything was on the system, and all we had to do was wait.

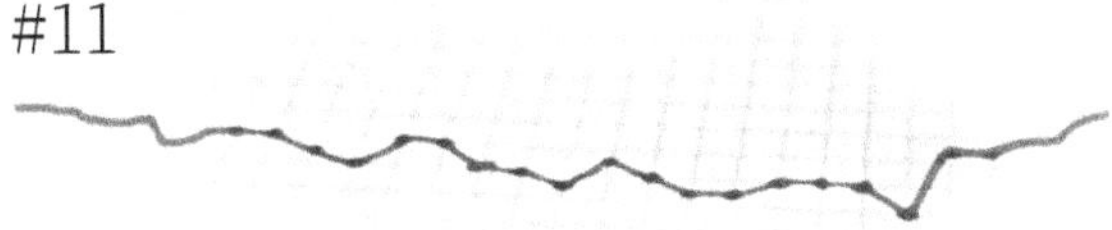

We can finally see the specialist

I have been continuously checking the mailbox every single day for our new medical insurance cards. Finally, today they arrived; we have been waiting a month now. We are now finally ready to go and see the fertility specialist. Hopefully he can tell us what is wrong with us and how to proceed.

I have also informed Mrs. Melber that we now have Bituach Leumi, and she told me to make an appointment with a Dr. Dior in a place called Beit Egged. She told me it can take up to two months till he's available, but he is the best doctor there. She also said we could go to other doctors if we wanted, and she gave us a few different names. I called up Beit Egged and asked for the earliest appointment with Dr. Dior. To my surprise, they said one was available next week, as they just had a cancellation. I booked it and put it in my calendar.

Etty and I are feeling nervous about seeing him. What happens if he tells us we have a serious problem and we will never be able to have children naturally? On the other hand, we are also feeling more at ease since we now have some form of direction to go. We are thankfully able to see a specialist, and he will hopefully tell us what to do.

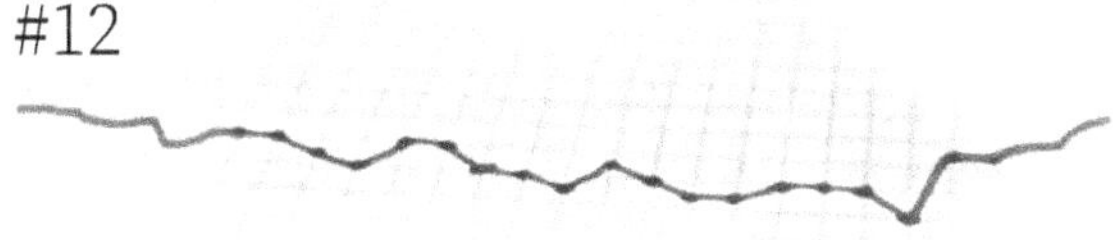

Pain of the unknown

We have been married for nearly one and a half years now. Many of our friends have already had babies, as well as cousins of mine who have gotten married either at similar times to us or just after us. They have already given birth or are currently very pregnant. Etty hates socializing with her married friends, because every time she sees her friends' babies, she thinks about how she could have also had a baby by now, or at the very least she should be pregnant. Every time Etty sees a buggy, it upsets her and ruins her day. She thinks to herself, *Why can't I have children? Have I done something wrong?*

These thoughts pop into my head too when seeing babies, but they are definitely not as prevalent as Etty's. What bothers me the most is when I hear people speaking about how unhappy they are with their children. All they do is complain about how their child is waking them up during the night and driving them crazy all day. I think to myself about how lucky they are and how that very thing that bothers them would make me so much happier. I know everyone says "the grass is always greener on the other side," but I really think it's terrible to be complaining about your children when there are so many people who are desperate for just that. Etty tells me the whole time, she wishes she can have a small baby crying at night to wake her up.

My mother is also asking me every so often what is going on, and if there have been any developments yet. I am happy to tell her, and she is happy to be kept in the know. Whereas Etty's parents haven't even said one word. It is getting a bit strange by now. Etty is wondering if they don't care at all if she is pregnant or not. She can be speaking to them on the phone about a certain friend who just had a baby, and they will say how nice it is and ask all sorts of questions, but they never mention one word about Etty not having a baby yet. Do they not want grandchildren? Do they not want to know how Etty is keeping and how she's holding up? Do they not want to know if she's emotionally stable? It's almost as if they think it's perfectly normal to not be pregnant after trying to conceive for a year and a half.

Etty also doesn't have anyone to speak to about our situation, as she doesn't want to discuss it with any of her friends. They are either pregnant, or already have babies, and she doesn't feel comfortable talking to them. She wishes her mother would say something to her. I think I understand her mother, as she probably doesn't want to pry and be a "bad mother-in-law," but on the other hand, Etty really needs someone to talk to. She is bottling up all of her emotions, and that cannot be healthy.

We recently went back to our parents' homes abroad for *Yom Tov* (Jewish holiday), my mother approached me privately and told me that Aliza, who had gotten married before me and had had a child ten months later, was thinking about having another child, but she had said she felt weird having one if Etty was not yet pregnant. I told her that it's completely fine, and I have nothing to do with my sister having a child or not, and I really didn't mind. I was even a bit happy that someone realized what me might feel like and that someone was caring about our feelings. Later that evening, I found myself alone with my sister. She was walking down the stairs, and I met her on the landing. I told her, "Mummy spoke to me about you having another child, and I'm really happy for you." I also told her that she shouldn't have any feelings of guilt about becoming pregnant again, even though Etty was not yet pregnant. I ended by telling her that I would be more than happy to have another niece or nephew. The conversation was a bit awkward, but I was happy to have gotten it out of the way, and she seemed a bit relieved.

At the same time I was back home, my little sister Racheli, who is eight years old, asked me when I'm having a baby and why Etty wasn't pregnant yet. I told her that I don't know when it will happen, and she should *daven* (pray) to *Hashem* (God) for us. I was really upset that day; even my little eight-year-old sister has noticed something is wrong. Imagine what others are talking about behind our backs. I can't stop thinking about what we have done wrong, and why Hashem is punishing us like this. There are many other people in the world who are actually bad people, but their lives seem to work out fine for them. Why us? What did we do wrong?

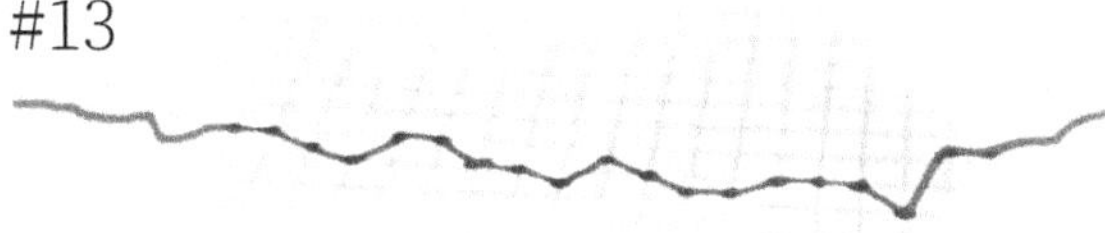

Dr. Dior

We arrived at Beit Egged today in time for our appointment and were informed that Dr. Dior was running half an hour behind schedule. We soon realized that Beit Egged was mainly used for fertility and female medical problems, as well as anything pregnancy-related. We hoped not to see anyone we knew while we were waiting, as they would wonder what we were doing here. We were not pregnant, and it would be as if we were telling them that we are having trouble. Thinking about it now, I realize how stupid it sounds, as everyone we know was obviously aware that something was up with us. We have been married one and a half years now, and we are still not pregnant. As Orthodox Jews, we have a commandment to have children, so the majority will have at least one child immediately after getting married, and then some may wait a while to have another, but others will have other children straight after their first. Our minds play funny tricks on us, especially when people are emotionally vulnerable, and all sorts of negative thoughts are constantly popping into our heads, such as maybe we are doing something wrong by not being pregnant, even though it's not at all in our hands.

Eventually, Dr. Dior was ready to see us, so we went into his room. He sat us down, looked at all our blood test results and my sperm test. He said that everything was completely fine with us, and there was nothing he can see that's out of the ordinary. I asked him if we should be here, as everything was fine, so he explained that if someone has been trying to conceive for over a year without success, it must mean they are experiencing some form of infertility. In our case, there was nothing that could be pointed to as being the underlying cause of the problem, so he diagnosed us with unexplained infertility. He told us how unexplained infertility is a real problem; he explained that although science is extremely developed, they still don't know how many things work with regards to becoming pregnant. So unexplained infertility is like saying, "You have a problem; something is not right. We know what it's not, but we don't know what it is." He told us 25 percent of infertility cases are unexplained.

He also told us they use the same methods of treatment to treat unexplained infertility as they do to treat other types of infertility, so Etty will be taking different hormone medications, which will hopefully improve her chance of becoming pregnant. He assured us that even though they don't know what is wrong with us, most of the time, the treatments are successful, and we should not think that we will never have children. But it is still important to do something about our situation.

He explained the first method he will use to try help us conceive. It is called IUI (intrauterine insemination). What they do is as follows. They take my semen, remove all the extra secretions, and concentrate the sperm. They then take the sperm and inject it directly into the uterus through the cervix. By doing this, they bypass any problems that could arise along the way until the sperm reaches the fallopian tubes, as well as increasing the actual sperm count that reaches the fallopian tubes. Then hopefully, at least one of the sperm will penetrate Etty's egg and fertilize it. He also told us Etty will be taking hormone pills called Letrozole, which should stimulate the ovaries and will help produce better eggs.

He then introduced us to the nurses at Beit Egged who will be dealing directly with us and will be liaising with him. He bid us farewell and once again assured us that we will definitely have children.

We spoke to the nurses, who were really nice and explained to us how everything will work. Etty will need to come in the next time she gets her period and have an internal ultrasound scan and blood test. The scan will determine how many eggs are currently in the fallopian tubes, as well as what size they are, thereby estimating when ovulation will be. The blood test will help determine the hormone levels, also helping them decide when Etty will ovulate. Once they know when ovulation will be, the two nights before her ovulation, we must refrain from sleeping together, and then that morning, I will need to take my semen to the local hospital, where it will be refined and then injected through Etty's cervix.

They also told us that the blood tests need to be done before eight thirty a.m., so that they can have the results that afternoon. They advised Etty to take the ultrasound scan at the same time she takes the blood test, because it's more convenient, and she will need to come to the nurses and give them the scan results. They showed us where everything was and told us we can call them if we need anything, or had any questions.

We are now feeling really hopeful. We feel confident that we are in good hands and everything will work out well. Etty is a bit nervous to take all the medication, as there are different side effects, such as facial bloating and sudden mood swings, but she is happy that we are finally doing something about our problem. We are now both waiting for Etty to get her period, so we can start with the treatment. I think this time when her period comes, we will be happy as opposed to sad, how we usually feel, because it is a sign that we can actually start trying to fix the problem, and we won't look at it as another failure.

#14

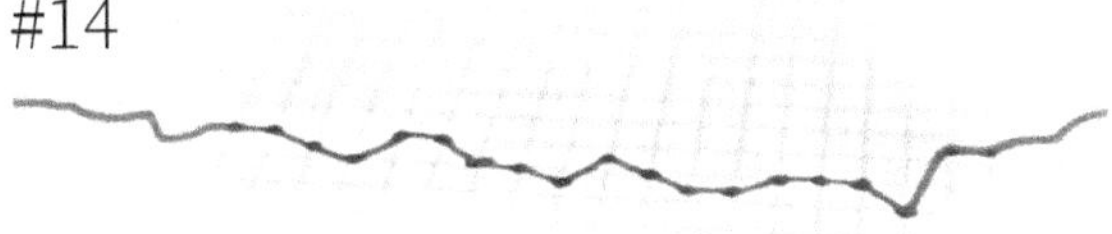

Blood tests and ultrasounds

Two weeks ago, Etty got her period. On day two of her period, we woke up earlier than usual and arranged to get to Beit Egged at seven thirty a.m. to do the ultrasound scan and blood test. When we got there, we were surprised to see how long the line was. We took a number and waited till it was our turn. Eventually we were called, so we entered the room and gave the nurse our referral. Etty was told to lie down on the bed. The woman took the machine and did an internal ultrasound. Etty looked really uncomfortable; her face was contorted, and she kept on asking the woman if it was over yet. She was breathing extremely heavily, and I was feeling really anxious just looking at her face. The woman told her to calm down, and everything would be okay. She told Etty that if she calms down and doesn't move, it won't hurt.

There was a big screen on the wall with a live video feed of what was going on inside. It was mostly black, with a few different gray shades and some circular shades of a whitish-gray color. The nurse explained that those circular shapes were the follicles, which she then started measuring. We learned that once the follicle gets to around twenty centimeters, it means it's ready to ovulate. We also learned that there may be a few follicles showing up on the screen, but that does not mean that all of them will ovulate or even continue growing.

After the scan, we got a printout of the results and went upstairs to get a blood test. The line there was also extremely long, so we sat down to wait. A while later, it was our turn, so Etty went in to get her blood test done, and then we went to line up by the nurses. Finally, it was our turn. We went in and gave the nurse the ultrasound results. She said everything looked fine and someone would call us later that afternoon with the blood test results, telling us what to do next.

We got home at around nine a.m.; I had to quickly eat breakfast and rush to my yeshivah. At around one thirty p.m. that day, I got a call from Beit Egged, saying everything was fine, Etty should start taking the Letrozole tablets, and she should come in again two days later. The next time we went in, we decided to go super early; this way we won't need to wait in line that long and would be able to get it all over and done with in thirty minutes. So for the past two weeks, every second day, Etty has woken up at six thirty a.m., got to Beit Egged at seven a.m., had an internal ultrasound scan as well as a blood test, and was back home at a quarter to eight.

All this waking up early, waiting till the afternoon for the phone call, and Etty having to take ultrasound scans and blood tests has really had an emotional and stressful toll on us. Firstly, Etty is only getting a six-hour sleep as opposed to her usual eight hours. Secondly, Etty hates all the scans and still hasn't stopped feeling uncomfortable during them. Thirdly, I am literally waiting all morning for my phone to ring and can't really focus on anything I'm meant to be doing. We are both worried every morning until we get that phone call. What happens if they call and say something is wrong with Etty's hormone levels? We may have to start again, or maybe even do something more painful.

I know plenty of people wake up super early, but I don't think anyone should ever be in a situation where it is normal for them to be pricked with a needle daily, as well as having uncomfortable ultrasounds. But unfortunately, this has become Etty's life, and who knows how long it will continue?

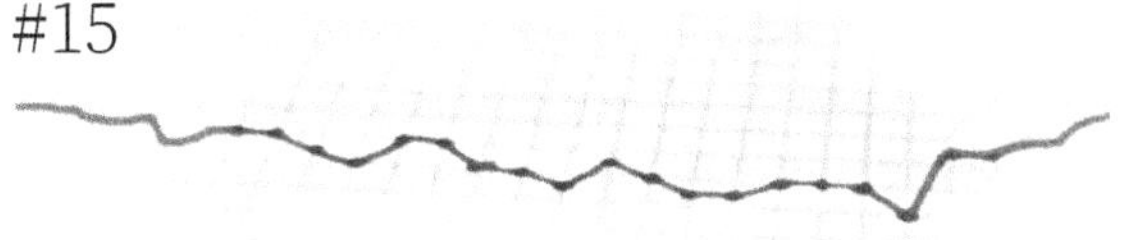

Doing IUI (Intrauterine Insemination)

Two days ago, we received the phone call from Beit Egged that Etty was ovulating. They instructed us not to sleep together the next two nights, and on the morning of the ovulation day, we should bring my semen to Bikur Choilim Hospital and give it to the lab there. Once again, everything had to be done within an hour, and before eight thirty a.m. We got to the hospital at eight a.m. today and handed over my semen. They were extremely careful with labeling it, making sure it won't get mixed up with anyone else's, and told us to come back in an hour and a half.

After ninety minutes, we were shown into a room that had a desk and a bed. The nurse told Etty to lie on the bed. They then took a metal clamp, which they used to open up Etty's vagina, so they could see what's going on inside. Etty looked very uncomfortable with her face contorted and was breathing really heavily. She was telling me that this was much worse than an internal ultrasound scan, and I was trying to console her, telling her that it will all be over in a few minutes. They then took my refined sperm from the test tube and poured it into a syringe, which had the longest needle I have ever seen in my life attached to it, which ensured that the sperm got ejected all the way up through the cervix to the fallopian tubes. The whole process took around two minutes, but Etty felt like it was hours. The nurse doing it didn't actually say anything and just did it as if nothing was happening. I suppose he probably does this many times a day, but he could have said something to help Etty calm down. He then removed all the equipment and told Etty to stay on the bed for the next ten minutes. Ten minutes later, she got off the bed, and we left the hospital.

There is nothing more for us to do now besides wait patiently for Etty to become pregnant. We are both extremely happy it is now all over and we can continue with our normal lives. Hopefully, Etty will become pregnant, as everyone keeps on telling us, "There is nothing wrong with you, and there is no reason why IUI shouldn't work."

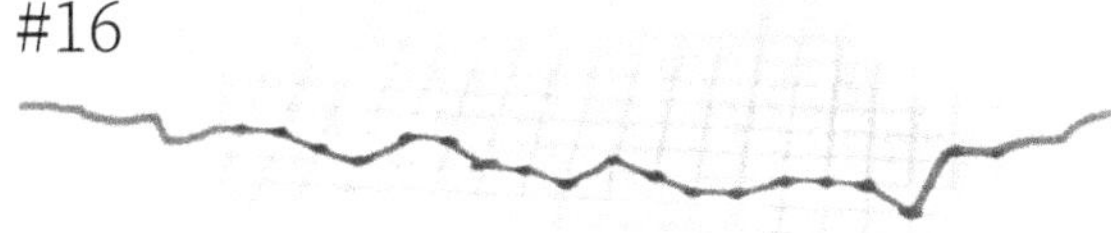

It failed

I'm feeling devastated; I feel like the world has ended. Etty has been crying for the past hour, and I am feeling extremely down. I'm in a really bad mood and don't really want to talk to anyone at the moment, but I need to go look after my wife. Etty got her period today. How could IUI not have worked? Etty thinks maybe it's because she didn't stay long enough on the bed after IUI. But I'm trying to tell her that it's not her fault and she shouldn't blame herself. I have sent a message to Mrs. Melber, telling her it didn't work, and I called Beit Egged, letting them know too.

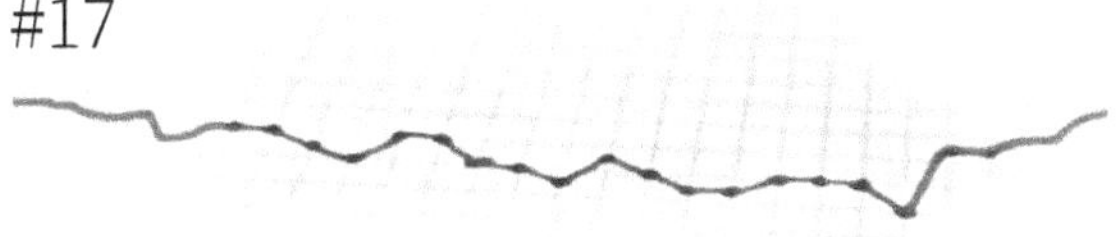

Pain, anguish, and no hope

Today is one year after we went to visit one of the *Gedolim* (great rabbi of the generation) to get a brocha (blessing) from him. A year ago, we went to Bnei Berak to ask for a brocha. It was really interesting there, and he received us really warmly. We told him we didn't have children yet, after being married for a year. So, he gave us a beautiful brocha, saying within a year, Etty will be pregnant. We thanked him and left Bnei Berak, feeling happy and relieved.

But today I'm at a loss; Etty is still not pregnant. We are both devastated. How could one of the Gedolims' brocha not work? What have we done so bad already? I know and understand that just because someone gives you a brocha, it doesn't mean that it will happen. But I am finding it extremely hard to realize that. I have made a mental resolve that from now on, I am not going to go around anymore asking for brochas.

It's easy to think, "Why not? A brocha can't harm you." In fact, my parents have told me this very thing numerous times. But I just can't face going through all the excitement again and waiting for the brocha to come true, only to be let down later. It's too emotionally heartbreaking for me; I feel like I'm broken now. Telling me not to have such high hopes and get a brocha anyway still won't work. I feel so desperate, and we want children so badly, that anything I can grasp on to is blown up in my mind, and the letdown feels awful and is too much for us to handle.

I also feel exactly the same way with *segulas* (protective, benevolent charm, or ritual in Kabbalistic and Talmudic tradition). My rabbi has given me numerous segulas to do. Many of them come from real sources, and we have done them all, but still nothing happens. The segulas have included, saying *Asher Yotzar* (blessing said after being excused) with *kavona* (intent), saying *Tefilas Chanah* (a certain prayer a woman called Chanah said, asking God to give her children, and that night she became pregnant) after lightning candles on Friday night, saying the whole *Sefer Tehillim* (book of Psalms) without any breaks (which took me three hours and was extremely difficult), and many more. Therefore, I have stopped doing segulas, as once again, the emotional high I get from doing them out of desperation creates awful and horrible feelings when months later Etty is still not pregnant.

Another thing that unfortunately Etty and I are constantly finding harder and harder to do is daven (pray) to Hashem for children. It's not that we don't believe in Him. On the contrary, we are big believers, and I still ask Him for many other things, and we see His hand in our day-to-day life (for example, if Etty's business is not going well, she will pray and give tzedoka (charity), and the next week, it's much better). But I have been asking for children since I was seventeen, and I have been asking even more intently since our first wedding anniversary. Yet every single month, when Etty gets her period, we feel extremely let down. I have sort of come to the conclusion that He doesn't want us to have children at the moment, for whatever reason, and when the time is right, He will give them to us. But I have stopped asking Him for them, as He definitely knows what we want. Etty always tells me, "I feel like a beggar asking Hashem every single day for the same thing, only to be rejected at the end of every month." I answer her that her feelings are valid and I feel the same way, and whenever He thinks it's the right time, we will have children anyway. We sometimes also feel a bit homeless and unwanted, by constantly asking Hashem for children and then being constantly rejected.

Another thing that is constantly setting off our emotions is Etty getting her period. My rabbi tells me it's amazing that we get upset every month, as it shows we still have hope and haven't given up yet. But I find it awful to watch Etty crying every time she tells me she has her period, and I can't even give her a hug or kiss, since in Jewish law, once a woman receives her period she becomes impure, and the couple can't sleep together or touch each other until the woman goes to mikvah (a ritual bath). When that happens, I am usually in a bad mood for the rest of the day, sometimes even letting out my anger on poor Etty.

Besides for the period signaling that Etty is not pregnant, it's also telling us that any medication we have taken was a waste of time and that we will have to start all over again in two days' time. Imagine having worked on something for a month, taking medication, feeling unwell, being pricked daily, and having extremely uncomfortable procedures done to you—only to realize two weeks later, that everything was a complete waste, and it didn't even help. I really don't think anyone should ever have to go through this. Etty doesn't really show her emotions; she usually gets all quiet and reserved, and I only know when she is upset when she starts crying. But she always talks about how it's another month of not being pregnant and another month of having to walk around without a baby, with people looking at her, wondering what is wrong.

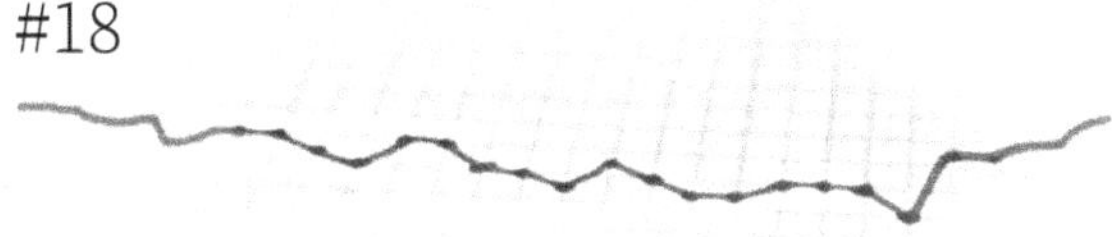

18

Injections

Etty got her period two days ago, so we woke up early again today and went back to Beit Egged. After taking the internal ultrasound scan and having the blood test, we went to see the nurses. They informed us that they had spoken to Dr. Dior, and he had said it was time to step up the procedures.

They introduced us to a hormone injection called Gonal F, showing us something that looked like an EpiPen. Every evening, Etty will need to inject herself with this pen, which will give her hormones a boost, stimulating her ovaries, resulting in stronger and bigger eggs. They informed us of the side effects, which include mood swings and facial bloating; anything worse than that and we would need to go to the hospital. They also made us sign a paper saying that if we manage to become pregnant, but there are more than two fertilized eggs, we will have an abortion, as it is considered a high-risk pregnancy. I'm still not sure exactly how I feel about signing the paper. On the one hand, we want children, and if Etty becomes pregnant with three babies, then I would be more than happy to have three children. On the other hand, I understand that it is a high-risk pregnancy and can be dangerous. But then again, I know many people who have given birth to triplets. So I'm feeling a bit unsure about this, but it's not like we have much of a choice. If we don't sign it, they won't let us continue with the treatment.

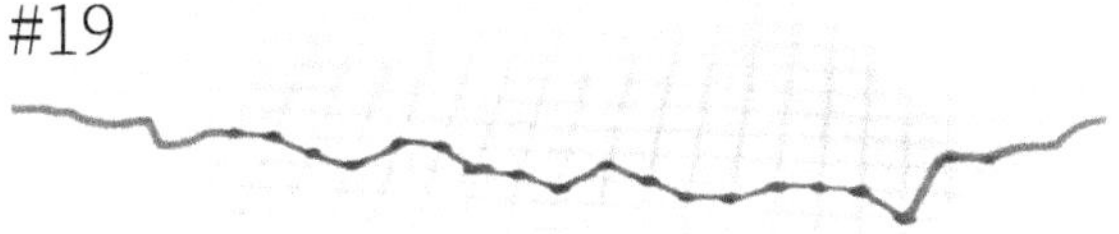

19

Waking up early yet again

For the past two weeks, Etty has once again been going every second morning to get an internal ultrasound scan and blood test. Every afternoon, they have called us with the results, and that evening, Etty has injected herself with the hormones. The injection has to take place just below her navel. Sometimes she bleeds from it and sometimes she doesn't. I asked my rabbi if she can do it on *Shabbos* (Sabbath/Saturday), and he confirmed that she could, as it is not definite that she will bleed.

Two days ago, they called us up and said Etty was ovulating in two days' time. They told us to stop with the injections and not be together for the next two nights. On the second morning, we would have to do IUI again, going through exactly the same procedure as last time.

So today we did IUI again, and this time Etty made sure to stay on the bed for longer than ten minutes after the procedure. I really hope this time it will work. I really hate watching Etty inject herself every evening, and I hope this will be the last time she needs to do it.

#20

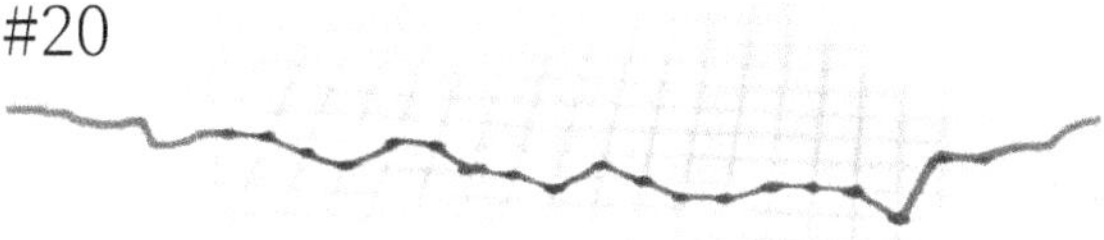

Another failure

Today Etty got her period again. We are both devastated. All those early mornings, all those ultrasounds and blood tests, and all the injections, all for nothing! I we really thought this time it would work. Now we have to start all over again. Is this going to be our life for the foreseeable future? I have informed Mrs. Melber and called up Beit Egged. They told us to come back in two days' time.

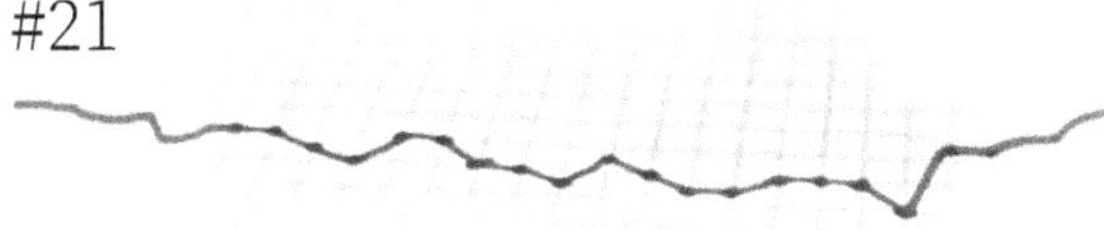

21

The third IUI

Today we woke up early again and went to have the ultrasound scan and blood tests. When we got to the nurses, they told us once again that Dr. Dior had upped the treatment. This time they were introducing another injection called Ovitrelle. Etty has to inject herself with it the day before we do IUI. It makes the ovulation more precise, as well as somehow improving it. So we have once again started the whole procedure, waking up early, having daily internal ultrasounds and blood tests, as well as Etty injecting herself with hormones every evening.

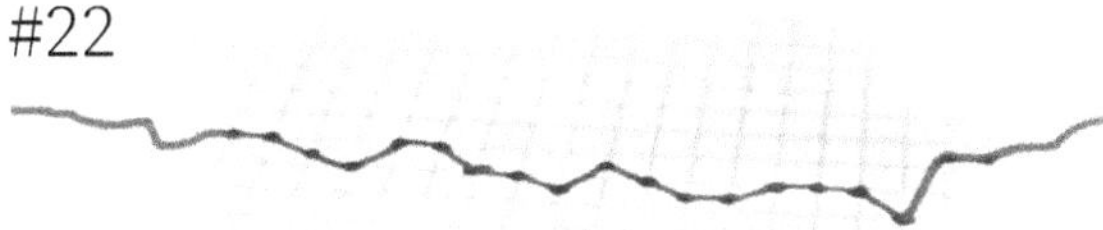

22

Ovulation

Two days ago, they called us and said Etty was ovulating in two days' time, and we should once again not be together for the next two nights. The evening before IUI (which was yesterday), she should inject herself with Ovitrelle. Today we went back to the hospital and did IUI for the third time. Once again, we are both extremely hopeful and think this month it will work. This month, Etty will become pregnant!

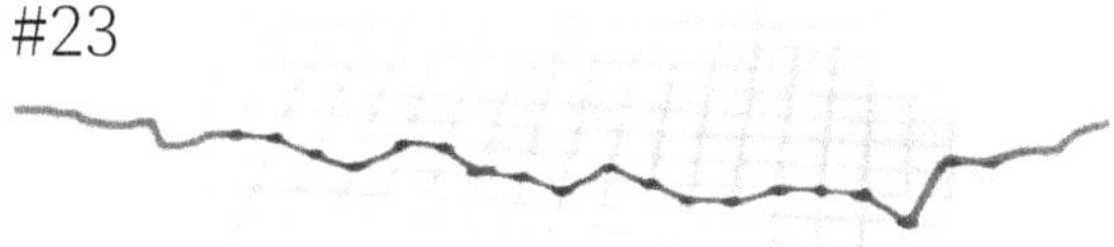

23

Yet another period

Once again, Etty got her period today, and we are devastated again. What a waste of getting up early, Etty injecting herself, and going through really uncomfortable procedures. Why is it not working? This time we even used Ovitrelle. Is that really not enough? What are we meant to do? How long will this take already?

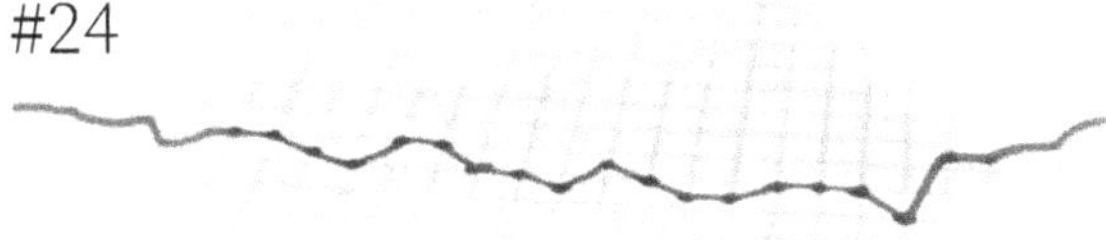

24

The sixth failure

Today, Etty got her period again. We have already done IUI six times now. Every single month, they have been intensifying the hormone injections. Etty has been waking up early, having internal ultrasounds and blood tests, and two weeks later, we do IUI. It has always resulted in Etty getting her period and us feeling extremely rejected and down.

We have already done IUI six times over the past nine or so months. They have not always back to back, as sometimes we have gone back to our homes abroad, sometimes we took a break for a month or two, and sometimes there were technical difficulties, so we just couldn't do it that month.

Many times, Etty's period came late, sometimes even two weeks late. We would get so excited and think she was pregnant. Although Etty doesn't like to get too happy, as she hates being let down, I always think, *this time it worked!* A few times, we even took pregnancy blood tests to confirm the pregnancy, but each time they come back negative.

Our world is being shattered before our eyes. We always ask each other what we have done wrong. I constantly ask Etty, "Are we really such bad people? I know so many other people that are as religious as us, yet they don't seem to have any problem having children, and just pop them out every other year or so. Why us?" Sometimes we even blame ourselves for things we have done in our pasts. (Not that we think we are bad people, but we think about the few times we remember doing something wrong and use that as a reason why we are being punished.) But Etty always tells me that I'm not a bad person. She points out all the good we do and tells me she knows people who are much worse than us, yet they have become pregnant straight after getting married.

I think we have started to realize that we won't have children anytime soon and have started to accept the fact that we are different from everyone else. But we will never give up hope, and we're still being triggered by stupid things, such as newborn babies. Every now and again, Etty will come home crying because she just saw a young mother pushing a baby around in a buggy, and she wonders why she doesn't have children yet.

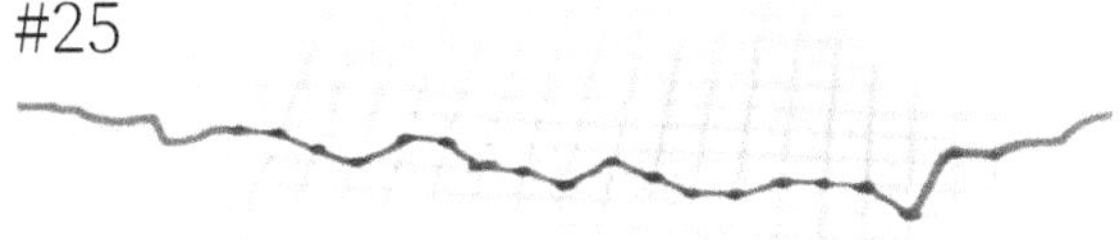

25

Not being understood

Today Etty decided to ask her mother why she hasn't said anything to her yet about not being pregnant. It was an interesting conversation, and unfortunately it didn't go as Etty had planned. Her mother said, "Why are you so nervous and scared about it? Me and Daddy waited three years till we had you, and don't worry. I'm sure there is nothing wrong with you. I was in the same situation as you, and I'm sure you will get over it and have children soon."

Etty also told her mother that we have been seeing doctors and getting treatment for our unexplained infertility. Her mother replied, "Are you sure you really need to see doctors, especially if they keep on telling you that there is nothing wrong with you? I'm sure you will have a child soon. Me and Daddy only had you after three years, and we didn't need to do any treatment."

I also decided to speak to my father-in-law today about our situation. But it didn't go as I had planned either. He said, "I really don't think it's necessary to see any doctors. We have Hashem on our side, and all we need to do is daven to him. I'm sure you will have children really soon, especially if there is nothing wrong with Etty. My rabbi waited nearly ten years to have children, and he ended up having a child in the end. I also don't think that anyone should be doing any medical treatment unless you have been waiting for five years or more."

I answered, "My rabbi told me to do it, as well as all the professional and knowledgeable doctors in the field. So we cannot be crazy."

He said, "I don't think you're crazy. I just don't think it is necessary."

So, all in all, our conversations didn't go that well at all. Etty and I didn't expect that to happen, and I don't think I agree with my father-in-law about not seeking medical help yet. On the other hand, maybe he is right and a Jew shouldn't be doing anything medical related. Rather, we should be relying on God to fix our problems. I'm not sure what to think. I will speak to my rabbi tomorrow.

26

Getting clarification

Today I went and spoke to my rabbi about the whole situation. I told him about the conversation I had yesterday with my father-in-law. He said, "In Judaism, there are many different views. Some people believe that one shouldn't see any doctors and should just leave everything in the hands of Hashem. But we don't do that. We don't believe in miracles, and we believe that we should do everything in our power to fix the problems we have. Obviously, we need to daven and ask Hashem to help us, but we still need to do our part. I actually just spoke to someone who is really knowledgeable in the area of infertility, and he said, 'Nowadays, if a couple is not pregnant after nine months, then they should go and seek medical help.'"

So I'm really happy that we are not making a mistake and I'm not doing something wrong. But I'm still finding it difficult to understand why my father-in-law believes what he said. I suppose every person is entitled to their own beliefs.

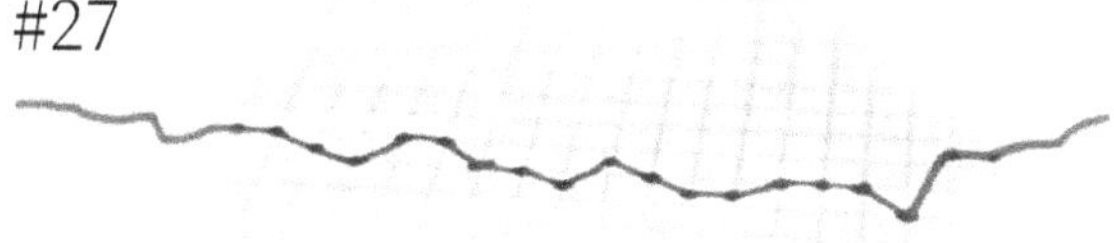

27

Finding someone to talk to

Today Etty received a random text from a cousin of hers whom she hardly ever speaks to. She is much older than Etty and is actually going through secondary infertility. The text said, "Hi, how are you? If you want, you can ignore this message and make as if you never received it. I realize that you may be going through something similar to me, and if you ever want to talk about it, I'm here for you." Etty was extremely touched; this was the first person who has actually noticed her, realized something was wrong, and was talking to her about it, as opposed to talking about her behind her back. But she doesn't feel comfortable talking to a cousin, especially one who is much older than her, and she doesn't really know her that well.

She replied to the text, thanking her for being in touch, telling her how touched she is, and assuring her that if she needs to talk to someone, she would message her.

I have been trying to convince Etty to talk to her, but she just says she doesn't feel comfortable. I told her how I think it's really important for her to talk to someone about her struggles, but she replied, "I hate talking about the situation. It just arouses all the negative feelings, and I definitely don't want to talk to a cousin that is ten years older than me."

Etty still doesn't have anyone to talk to about her feelings and struggles, besides for me. I have my Rabbi and my parents, but I think Etty really needs someone. It's awful to bottle everything up inside of yourself and not let it out, I am actually scared she will somehow burst. I really don't know what to do about it.

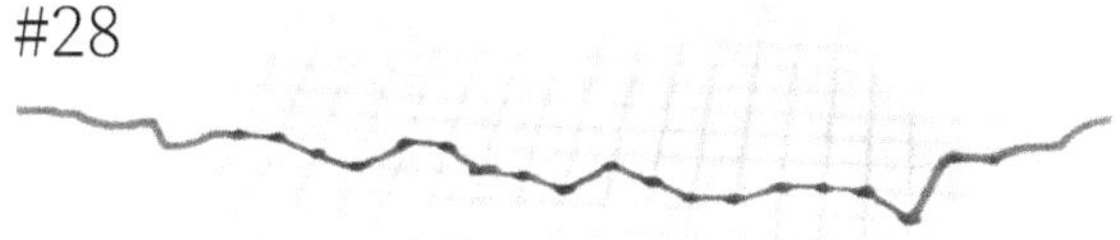

28

Etty must talk to someone

Today my rabbi told me that Etty has to speak to someone. He said it's not an option for her not to talk to anyone anymore, and if she doesn't find someone soon, he will set her up with someone he knows. I told this to Etty, and she understands why he said that, but she is still really uncomfortable about talking to someone. Nevertheless, she plucked up the courage and asked a lady who has given her some *shiurim* (Jewish lectures) recently, if she could make time to talk to her.

Thankfully the lady said yes. They will meet tomorrow at ten a.m. in her apartment. I'm feeling so relieved about it!

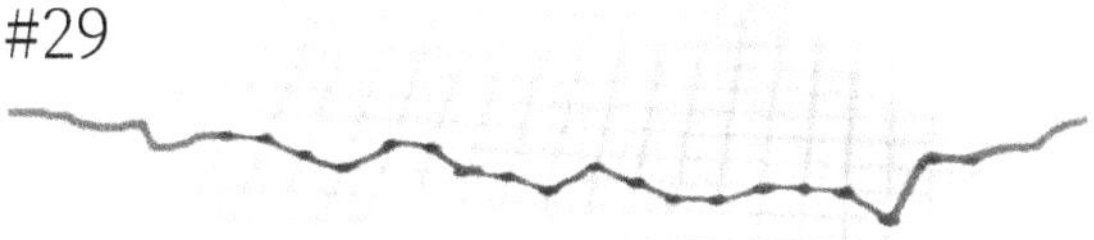

The meeting

Etty really loved the meeting today. She spent a full hour telling the woman about everything she has been going through the past two and a half years. When she got back and told me about it, I felt like a huge boulder had been lifted off Etty's back, and I'm extremely happy with the outcome.

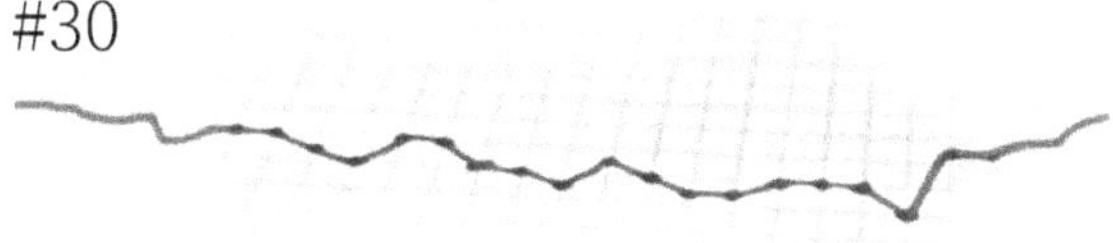

30

Another meeting

I was very surprised yesterday when Etty decided to contact the woman again and arrange a second meeting. Thankfully she was more than happy, and the meeting was arranged for today, the last one she had was a week ago.

It went really well, and Etty is a much happier person. The only downside is, this woman has never herself experienced infertility, so she is only a listening ear, as opposed to someone who can actually feel and understand Etty's struggles. But it is amazing that she has finally found someone to talk to. I'm really happy for her, and I'm feeling a bit less stressed too.

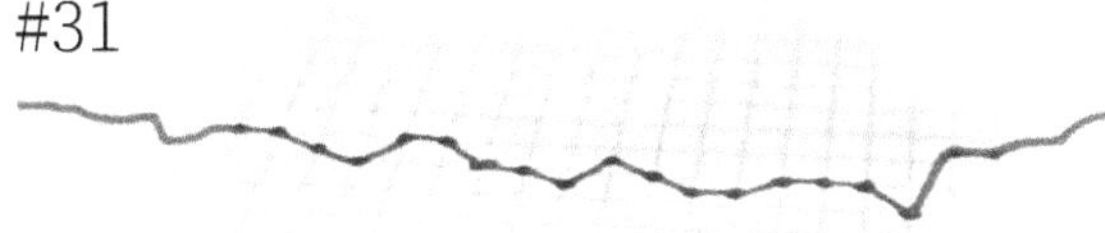

31

A friend

Today, when Etty was in Beit Egged, she met a good school friend there. They said hi awkwardly and did their own things. This friend got married at a similar time to us and also doesn't have children yet. When Etty got back home, she told me whom she had met and what had happened. I was elated. I told her that this was the chance she has been waiting for. Someone her age, someone she knew, and someone in a similar situation. Why doesn't she contact her and speak about it?

Etty felt really uncomfortable about it and immediately dismissed the idea. But I pushed her to send her friend a text message, using the same idea her cousin used to text her a few weeks ago. Telling her it's okay to ignore the message and about how she has been going to Beit Egged for the past year and a half. Finally, she agreed and sent the message. Only a few minutes went by, and she received a reply. The message said she was really happy that Etty had reached out, and she has been thinking about talking to her for a while now but didn't know how to broach the subject. They have organized a meeting time and will meet tomorrow over ice cream.

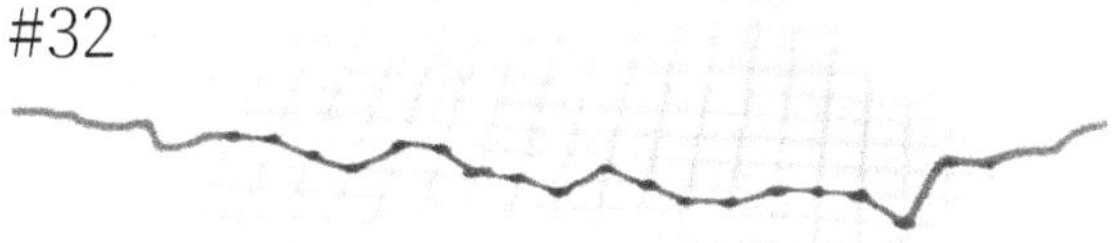

32

Someone who understands

Etty's meeting went really well today, and they spoke about every aspect of their struggles, really connecting with each other and sympathizing with their troubles. They both agree how hard it is to see their married relatives and friends with babies, as well as how any newborn is another trigger.

I am really happy it all worked out and Etty enjoyed every second of it, while being able to unload her emotional baggage to someone who understood her. They have arranged to have another get-together and to keep in touch. Finally she has someone she can connect to, who can understand her.

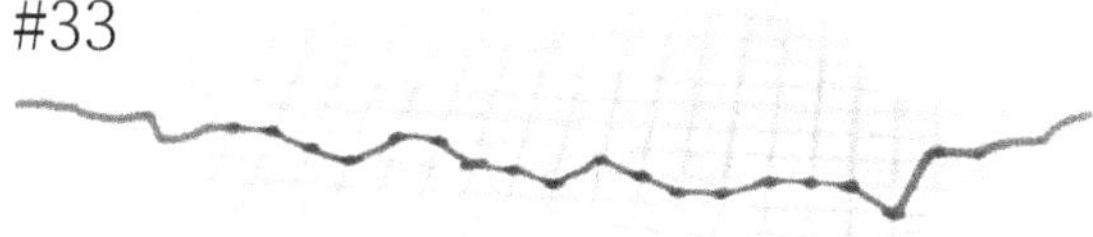

33

The HSG test

A few weeks ago, we went back to see Dr. Dior. We have already done IUI six times, and nothing has helped us. He explained to us that the next stage is doing IVF. He said that it is done at Haddassah Ein Kerem Hospital and not Beit Egged. He explained the procedure briefly but told us that in the hospital, they will explain everything much clearer. He also informed us that there are a few more tests we have to do before trying to apply for permission to do IVF.

The first test is called an HSG (hysterosalpingogram) test. The test is a special type of X-ray that looks at the shape of the uterus and assesses if either of the fallopian tubes is blocked, which would result in stopping the eggs ovulating properly. He told us the test is extremely unpleasant and is more invasive than anything else Etty has experienced before.

The only time we can have the test is after Etty's period has stopped but before she has ovulated. This only gives us a six or seven-day time period when the test can take place. So, I called up and booked an appointment. I was astonished to find out that they only did this test twice a week, and they had a one-and-a-half-month waiting list. So I booked the earliest available appointment, hoping for the best. They told me to call them when Etty gets her period in a month's time. Hopefully, if our appointment doesn't line up with the seven-day window, there would be a cancellation.

Three days ago, Etty got her period. It's a month after I booked the appointment, but I called them up and asked them if there was any availability. Thankfully, they had just received a cancellation and would be able to book us in for the test during the required seven-day window. The test was scheduled for seven thirty a.m. today, so we woke up early and arrived twenty minutes before the given appointment time. After waiting a while, they told Etty to enter a room and told me to wait outside. Only the person having the test and the person giving the test are allowed in the room; no one else can go in. Afterward, Etty explained what had gone on: first she lay on the bed, then they inserted a tube through her cervix, which sprayed a blue iodine solution into her uterus and fallopian tubes. She said it was extremely painful, as it was sprayed in at a high pressure, making sure the solution gets all the way up to the fallopian tubes. The nurse told her most times it causes internal bleeding, as the solution will often pierce the uterus lining. They then inserted a clamp into her just like IUI, which was followed by the X-ray tube.

The procedure took thirty minutes. Etty told me how awful and painful the test was, and she is happy it is over. She hopes to never need to do it again. Twenty minutes later, the nurse gave us a CD with the results, instructing us to give it to our doctor, so we dropped it off at Beit Egged on the way home.

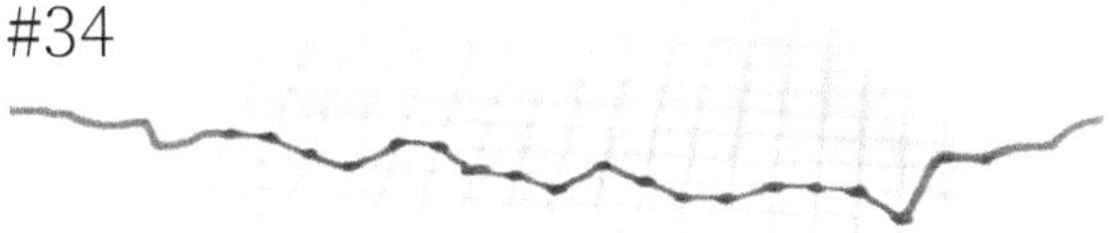

34

A panicked phone call

This morning, I received a phone call from a lady who sounded very panicky. She asked if our doctor had gotten back to us with the test results, as well as asking us if we had recently taken an internal ultrasound scan. I informed her that the doctor was not in for the next two days, and we had indeed had a recent ultrasound. I asked her if everything was okay with the results, to which she replied our doctor will tell us. I then called Mrs. Melber in a panic, telling her what had transpired. She asked me to go online, download the test results, and send them to her. After a while, she got back to me saying that everything seems fine to her, and there is absolutely nothing to worry about.

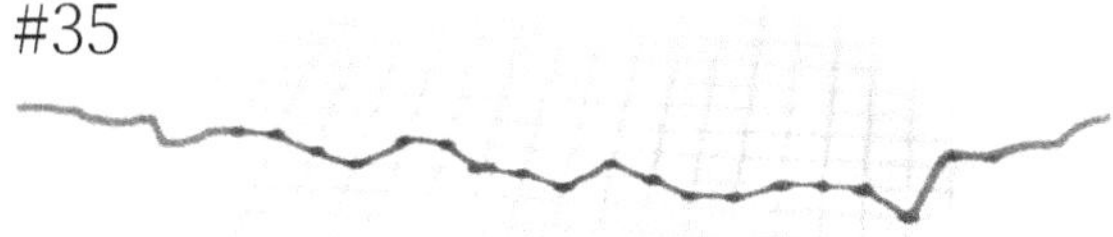

35

The results

Finally, the doctor called us today and informed us that from the HSG test, it looked like Etty has a cyst (a sac-like pocket of membranous tissue that contains fluid, air, or other substances; most cysts are noncancerous). But he said we shouldn't worry, as he can see from our most recent ultrasound scan, that it is only a leftover egg that never ovulated when it was meant to, and was definitely not a cyst. He said the egg should clear the next time Etty gets her period, and added that it is a very common thing to happen while taking hormone medication.

All these emotional ups and downs really don't do a whole lot of good to a human's mental health. First we were worried that something was wrong, then we felt relieved when Mrs. Melber told us it was fine. Only to get extremely worried when we heard the word *cyst*, and then again calming down when we heard it's nothing to worry about.

I don't think people realize that when it comes to infertility, there are so many different moments of emotional stress. Even if they only last for a few minutes, they are still very real. I have learned to never underestimate someone's emotions, especially when it comes to something as huge as becoming pregnant.

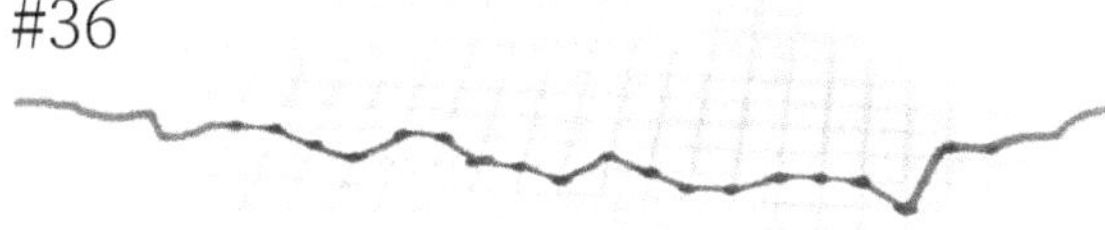

36

The next step

At our last appointment with Dr. Dior, we were told that we had to do a genetics test. This would make sure that we don't have any genetic defects that may be passed on to our future children. The reason they do this is because they don't want to go ahead with regular IVF if there may be a chance that the child will have some form of genetic deformity. Straight after the appointment, I called up to make an appointment and was shocked to hear that there was a six-month wait. I asked them if they have anything available sooner, even if it was in a different town. Thankfully, they had an available appointment in a few weeks' time. It was in Modin Illit, which is only an hour away from where we live.

Today was the day of the appointment. We got on the relevant bus and arrived in time and went to speak to the genetics nurse. She asked us a lot of questions about our ancestry and took seven tubes of blood from each of us. She then told us that the results will be available in a month. I'm not at all worried about this; there are no genetic problems in the family that I know of. It's just another one of the tests we have to do.

Pap test

Dr. Dior also told us Etty needed a Pap (smear) test. This tests for cervical cancer. Once again, they want to make sure Etty is perfectly healthy before giving us permission to do IVF. Today Etty had the Pap test, and it was better than Etty expected. We were informed that the results would be available in two weeks.

Finally, we have taken all the relevant tests. Now all we have to do is wait for the results and go to the hospital with them to do IVF.

#38

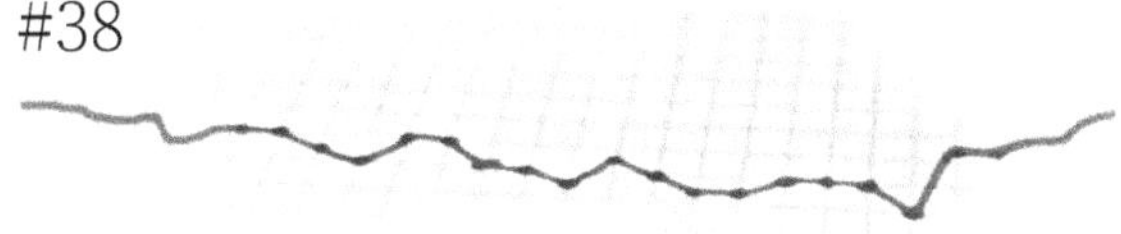

The same wavelength

I managed to arrange for my father-in-law to speak to my rabbi yesterday. My rabbi never told me exactly what they spoke about, but he said that my father-in-law was sorry, and he wants to start over again. He also added that my father-in-law suggested that we go daven by the Kosel (Western/Wailing Wall) every day for forty days, as he really thinks it will help us. I told my rabbi that I have finished doing *segulas* (protective, benevolent charm or ritual in Kabbalistic and Talmudic tradition), and he said he understood me, and was not telling me what to do; he was only passing on a message.

I am really relieved that I am now on the same wavelength as my in-laws, and they are happy we are going to doctors and seeking medical treatment. I have managed to forgive them and have put my feelings aside. Today was actually the first time we ever heard concern about our situation from them. In a passing conversation, my father-in-law told Etty that Mummy was really worried about her not being pregnant yet.

I'm thinking they are worried because we are at a different stage from what they were when they became pregnant. They had been pregnant after their second anniversary, and we are still not pregnant, and our third anniversary is around the corner.

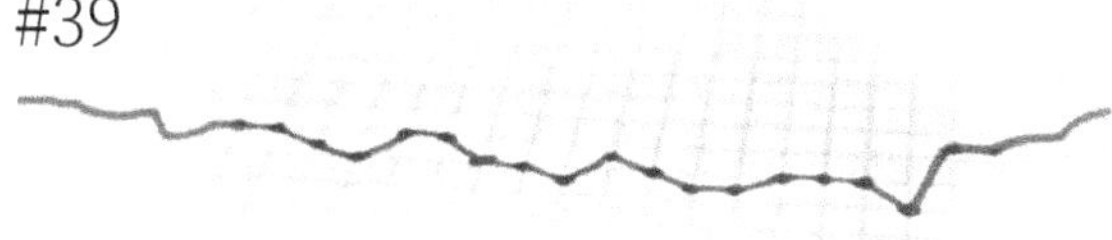

39

IVF

Once we had all the test results, we booked an appointment to open a new IVF file at the hospital. We had to wait a few weeks for our appointment. Finally, the appointment day has come, so we went to Hadassah Ein Kerem Hospital today for our IVF introduction. They opened up a file for us and explained to us how the whole procedure works.

On day two of Etty's period, we need to come to the hospital and take an internal ultrasound scan and blood test. Then they will call us in the afternoon, letting us know what dosage of hormone medication Etty should inject herself with for the next few days. The dosage will be much bigger than anything Etty has taken till now. Four days later, we will need to go back and take another ultrasound and blood test, and in the afternoon they will call us and tell us how much medication Etty needs to take for the next few days. Besides the usual hormone medication, Etty will also need to inject herself with a medication that stops her ovulating. After doing this for around two or three weeks, Etty should have at least ten to twenty large eggs waiting in the fallopian tubes. Usually people only have one egg every month, but for IVF, the most amount of eggs possible is needed.

When the eggs are ready, Etty will need to take the Ovitrelle injection, which will make her ovulate the next day. The next morning, we need to get to the hospital super early, and Etty has to prepare for a minor procedure. She will be put to sleep for around thirty minutes, and the doctor will use a needle-size instrument to suck out all of the eggs Etty has.

The same day, I will need to come in with my semen, which they will refine in the lab. Then later that day, they will take Etty's eggs and split them into two groups. Half of the eggs will have my sperm injected directly into them, and the other half will be put in close proximity to my sperm, letting the sperm naturally penetrate the eggs.

The next morning, any eggs that have not been fertilized are thrown away, and the rest of them are kept. They told us that usually around ten are successful. Then we will need to come back to the hospital, and they will transfer one of the embryos back through Etty's cervix, using the same method as IUI. They also told us we will have the choice of choosing to transfer one or two embryos. The rest of the embryos will be frozen to use at a later time. The embryo then has to implant itself onto the lining of the womb, and hopefully Etty will become pregnant.

After this, every day Etty has to take a number of tablets. Some of them need to be taken orally, and some of them need to be inserted like suppositories up to her cervix. These tablets give her progesterone and estrogen (hormones that are needed for pregnancy). The reason she needs to get these hormones through tablets is because the body doesn't think she is pregnant, as everything is done artificially, so it will not be producing enough progesterone and estrogen.

Two weeks later, Etty will need to go and have a pregnancy blood test, which will tell us if she is pregnant, and the embryo(s) have started to develop. If for some reason it doesn't work, and Etty is not pregnant, we can come back in the next month, and they will take another one of the frozen embryos out of the freezer and transfer that into her through the cervix. This way we won't need to go through all the hormone medication again.

All of this is a lot to take in, as well as their saying the side effects of all the medications are much bigger mood swings and much more swelling than anything Etty has experienced till now. I am also really confused and not sure if I should tell them to transfer one or two embryos. Maybe the only way we can have children is through IVF, and if that is the case, we want to have as many children as possible. Or maybe we just need to become pregnant once through IVF, and then we will be able to have children naturally. I have also been thinking about if I feel right 'playing God.' Who am I to decide how many children we will have?

The last thing they told us was that they have applied on our behalf to our medical insurance provider, for us to be covered for all the treatment. We are now full of hope and happiness that finally something will help us become pregnant.

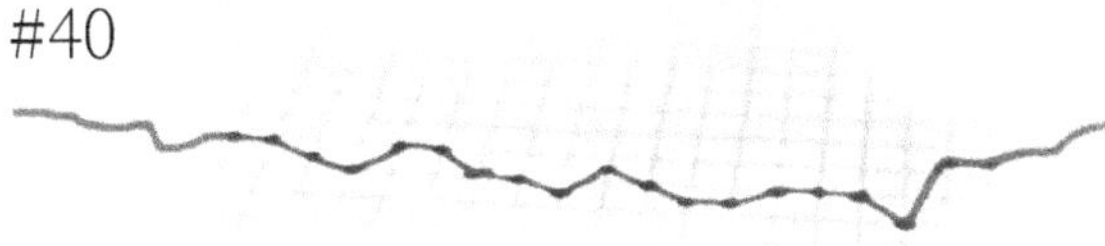

40

Another letdown

I contacted my health insurance today to see if we have been accepted for IVF. They informed me that we have been refused, as they have just changed the rules. Now, before being accepted for IVF we need to have done IUI six times, with hormone injections. Whereas we have done IUI six times, but the first time was without using any injections.

We feel devastated and don't know what to do. We are ready to do IVF, the doctors have told us it is the right time, but now it has been put on hold. I contacted Mrs. Melber, and she told me to talk to Dr. Dior and get him to try to push it through. So I have booked an appointment with him, but he is only free in two months' time, as he has gone away.

Mrs. Melber also said while we are waiting to see Dr. Dior, we might as well do another IUI. So the next time Etty gets her period, we will go back to Beit Egged.

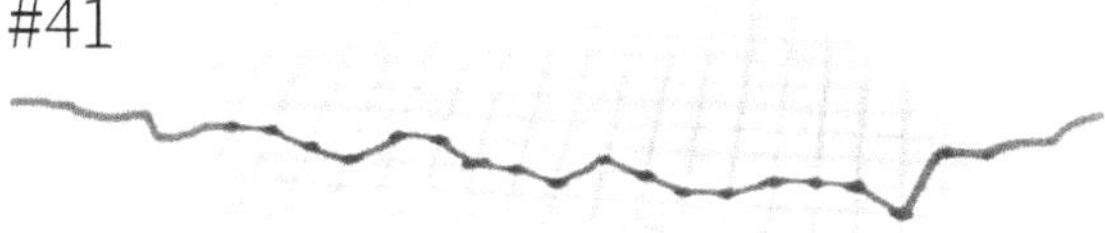

41

IUI once again

Etty started taking medication last week again so that we can do IUI once again, but today during the daily ultrasound scans, Etty noticed on the screen that there is more than one egg there. One time before, she has seen two eggs, but never as many as this time. She asked the nurses about this, and they said there are seven eggs that look big enough to potentially ovulate, so they will probably have to terminate this round. The lady doing the ultrasound had said she thought Etty was doing IVF, as there were so many eggs.

But to our surprise, when they called us this afternoon, they told Etty to take a higher dosage of the hormone injections, and they also upped the dosage for tomorrow. I hope they know what they are doing and everything is okay, but I assume they are experienced and know what to do.

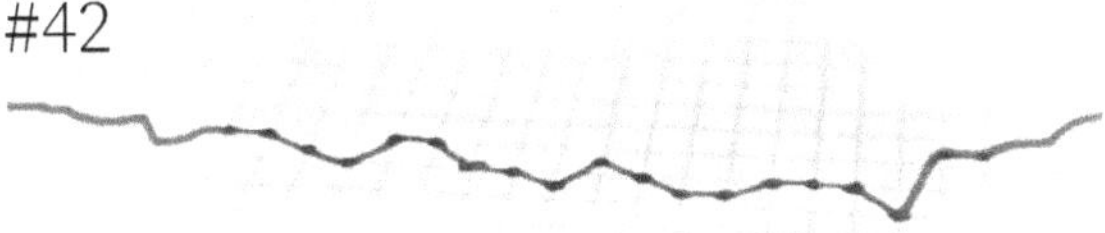

42

A mistake

Today the nurse called us and said that there had been some sort of mistake; the doctor who was telling what to do had somehow made a mistake. They said it wasn't our usual doctor, as Dr. Dior was currently away. They said Etty had way too many eggs, and getting pregnant now could be fatal, or at least extremely dangerous. This is known as ovarian hyperstimulation. So we have been told to stop everything and that we can't do IUI this month. They also told us that we can't be together for the rest of the month, just in case Etty becomes pregnant naturally.

We are really upset. What on earth is going on? Why is the doctor messing around with us? How can he be so careless and make such a mistake? We now have zero chance of becoming pregnant this month. It is really hard for us, as every month up until now we have felt there was a small sliver of hope, as it has been technically possible for us to become pregnant. But now, we have literally wasted an entire month. All the early mornings, all the injections, and all the medications—what a massive waste! I think this is the first time that we know for sure we can't become pregnant this month. It is such an awful feeling. It is as if our hands are tied behind our backs, and we are being told that nothing we do can help us. I don't think we have ever felt so helpless or lost before.

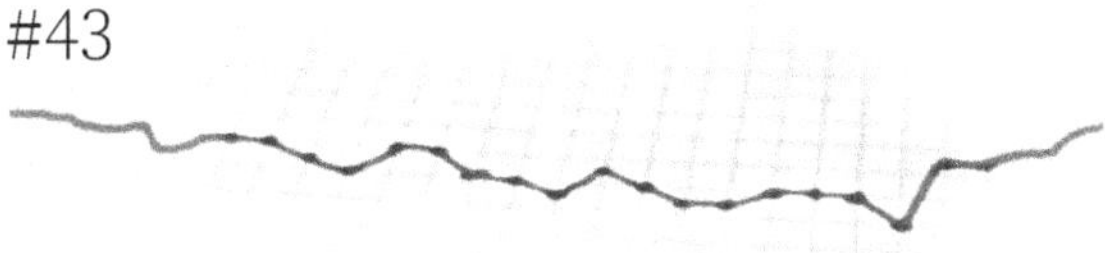

43

Back on track

We went to see Dr. Dior today. He was extremely surprised about what had happened the previous month and was also extremely upset that we had been refused permission for IVF.

There and then, he picked up the phone and called the head of our medical insurance provider. He gave him an earful and asked him what on earth he was thinking. The man informed him that he would give us permission for IVF, and it will be on the system by the end of the day. Dr. Dior also wrote us a letter in case the permission doesn't come through today, so we can use the letter to apply again.

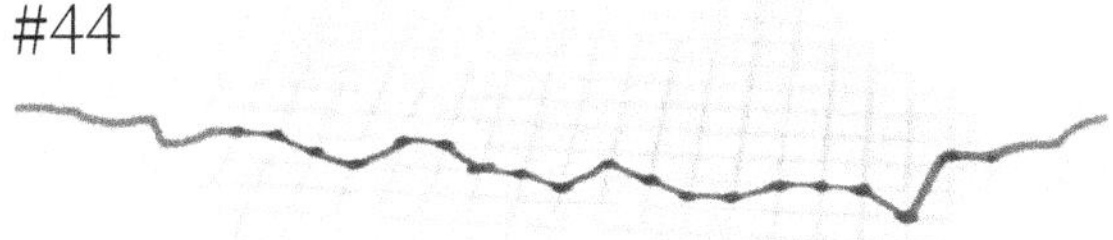

44

We have permission

I called this morning to see if we have been accepted for IVF, and was happy to hear that we had. It is nearing *Pesach* (Jewish holiday of Passover) now so we don't think we will have time to complete the IVF process before we leave Israel and go back to our homes abroad. Mrs. Melber has advised me to purchase the medication anyway, so that when we get back, we can jump straight into IVF, and won't need to wait around anymore.

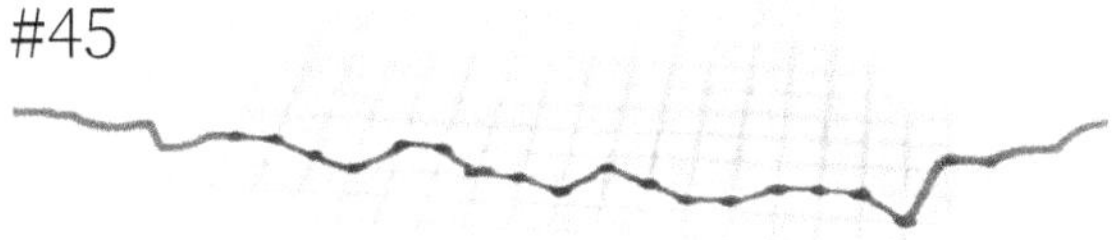

45

Purchasing the medication

I went to the pharmacy today to get the medication. I have never before purchased so many different types of injections and pills at the same time. The bill came to around 4,400 new Israeli shekel ($1,300 US), but thankfully we only had to pay for 10 percent of it, as our medical insurance covered the rest of it. I have put it all in the fridge until we get back to Israel.

#46

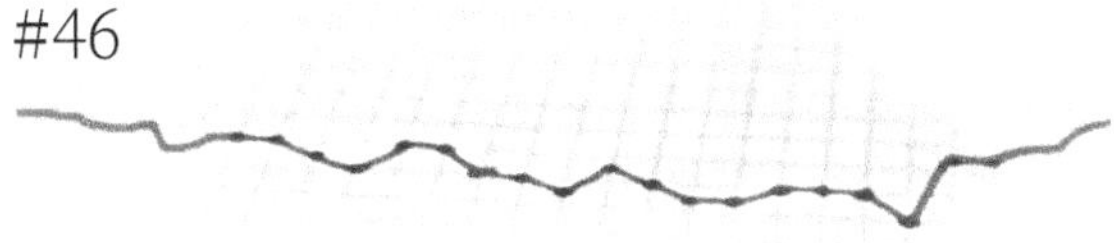

Anger and insensitivity

I attended a shiur today that was about the Halachik ramifications of using a surrogate mother. This is when the woman cannot become pregnant at all, so they transfer the couple's embryo into another woman to carry for nine months, and then the lady hands over the baby to the couple.

He explained the procedure of IVF, and I was shocked to hear that he had actually explained it incorrectly. There were many details missing, as well as details that were incorrect. I also noticed how insensitive he was when speaking about the topic. It was as if he was just discussing another daily occurrence, and how the whole process is a walk in the park.

Had this been directed at a group of great rabbis and being spoken about purely to understand what to do, then I would understand that it doesn't need to be of a sensitive nature. But this was a random shiur being given to random people, and the speaker had even started off by saying that he had just pulled the topic out of a hat.

Firstly, how can he give a shiur if he doesn't have all the facts right? Secondly, how can he speak about the whole topic of infertility and IVF without any feelings whatsoever? I'm sure I wasn't the only one sitting there who is experiencing infertility. Statistics say, one in fifteen people experience infertility, so there must have been at least one other person there with fertility problems, if not more.

It once again makes me realize that people really don't understand the difficulties of infertility and all the emotional baggage that comes with it. If he would truly understand that, I can't imagine he would have spoken about the topic with such cold feelings.

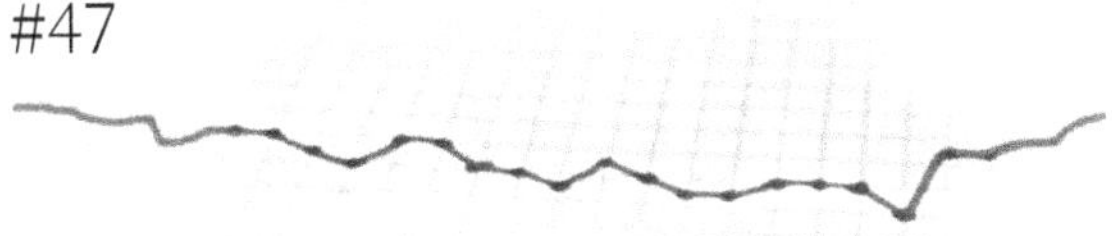

47

Anger and frustration

I just finished a call with my mother, and she told me that she had spoken to Aliza, who had said they had discussed Etty's and my infertility over Shabbos. Aliza said that they were sitting down at their Shabbos table Friday night, and one of the guests decided to start discussing who they knew who had already had children, and who they knew who didn't have children yet.

They discussed about how one person they knew had recently had a miscarriage, another person they knew was married for two years without children, and us, who have been married for nearly three years without children. The lady then continued to say, "Not to worry, I'm sure they will be doing IVF soon."

I told my mother, "This is absolutely disgusting. Firstly, why does anyone have the right to discuss other people's lives, especially something as personal as becoming pregnant? Secondly, they think that doing IVF is just a walk in the park. They don't realize about everything that has to be done before actually doing IVF, and they don't realize the cost of it if someone is not fully covered under their insurance. Not even mentioning all the side effects and emotional stress of not being pregnant, as well as having to take all the hormone medication." My mother agreed with me and said it was extremely insensitive of that woman, and Aliza had been shocked too, unsure of what to tell her. But she had felt it was important to tell me about it.

Thinking aloud, maybe it's important for me to share this diary with people, simply so that uninformed people will realize that

IVF is not just a walk in the park, and having fertility problems is extremely taxing on one's emotions.

Another thing that comes to mind is all the times people have said to me, "*Imirtsei Hashem* (with God's will) by you soon." What exactly do people mean by saying that? I know they think they are being nice and sweet. But to me it sounds like this: "Poor you, I know that you're having difficulties with becoming pregnant. Don't worry, though, you won't be a *nebech* (Yiddish word for a weak person, with strong undertones of pity and contempt) your whole life. Soon you'll have children."

All this does is serve as a reminder that I'm different from everyone else, and they look at me as a different person. I'm a normal person with unexplained infertility, and I don't need reminding of it every time I'm at a simcha (happy event) and am in a good mood. Every time someone says that to me, it reminds me of our infertility, and it ruins my day. I can't imagine I'm the only one who experiences this feeling. Rather, I think everyone who has fertility problems feels the same way.

The hardest emotional thing I think I ever went through was being *qvater* (the one who carries the baby) at a *bris* (circumcision). Don't get me wrong, it is definitely a beautiful thing to do by offering it to someone who doesn't yet have children. It is a known segula and is meant to work, causing one to conceive. But getting the phone call from my cousin asking me to be qvater at his son's bris was very hard for me. I felt like I was a true nebech and he was trying to help me. It was even worse when I walked into the *shul* (synagogue) caring the baby. I felt as if I was standing on a stage with a big sign hanging around my neck saying, "Look at me, I have fertility issues."

To top it all off, it was before Etty had gone to the mikvah, so we couldn't pass the baby to each other, so I had to give it to the mother of the child, who then passed it to Etty.

Thinking back, I don't know why we accepted it. We knew Etty had just gotten her period. I think the reason was because we were desperate. At the time, we were two years married, and I hadn't yet made my resolve to not do any more segulas. But we didn't realize what it would feel like to have all eyes on us, carrying the baby to the *mohel* (the person who perform the circumcision). I felt so awful that I didn't even want to take the baby back out afterward and tried to hide behind some people. But obviously they found me and told me I'm needed, which actually only made it much worse than me having just been there without all the commotion.

I'm not saying that people should never offer qvater to people they know who don't have children. Rather, they should think about it and how to best approach it. But I really don't know the best way to do it, though.

Another thing that has been very difficult for me was being *Chosen Kol Hanearim* (lit. groom who is the voice of the children. On the Jewish holiday of Simhat Torah, it is customary for every male to be called up to the Torah (Hebrew Bible) and recite a blessing. For children who are too young to read, someone will recite the blessings on their behalf. This is known as the Chosen Kol Hanearim) on *Succos* (Jewish holiday of Sukkot). My father arranged for me to get it, and I was extremely honored. But on the other hand, when I was standing there getting my *Aliya* (called up to the Torah) and saying the brochas (blessings), I felt extremely embarrassed. I felt once again like I was standing on a stage with a sign hanging around my neck, telling everyone I have fertility issues.

I don't know the right way to go about doing it, and I don't think people wouldn't want the segula. But I think it's important to realize what people go through, and about how difficult it is for us. On the one hand, we want the segulas, but on the other hand, we don't want to be standing on a stage embarrassing ourselves.

Another thing that really hurts my feelings and makes me realize once again that I'm a nebech is when people offer me advice or try to help me.

My father has a friend who has decided to take it upon himself to help us become pregnant. He has offered us endless advice, all the way from telling me to eat nuts and raisins every day to telling Etty to put a bucket of steaming water with rosemary under her and sit there for ten minutes, letting the steam clear up everything inside her cervix and womb, which will somehow improve our chances of becoming pregnant. These are the most ridiculous ideas I have ever heard. Does anyone really think that by eating certain foods or doing stupid things, it can really fix a problem that doctors have been trying to fix with scientifically proven things? I know he's just doing it for us and doesn't mean it in a bad way. But he's not a doctor, and he's not a rabbi. He doesn't even know us; he is just a friend of my father.

We did all these stupid things, but only to make my father happy. We didn't believe in them at all, and they didn't help us with anything. But my father was asking me if we followed his friend's advice, so we did it, as opposed to lying to my parents. While we were doing these stupid things, I was thinking to myself, *What on earth am I doing? Why am I wasting my time? Should I not just lie to my father and tell him we did it?* But I decided that lying is not good, and if we don't do them, he will tell us to try anyway, since it can't harm us. But I don't believe in all these Western-type medications and was happy to prove the point when they didn't help.

The worst part was when my father's friend met me on the street and asked me if we had managed to do them properly. What on earth was he thinking? Who does he think he is? Why would he ask me about my personal life. I didn't give him any indication that I wanted to talk about it with him.

I have also been advised by many others who think they are helpful, this one telling me to eat garlics, that one telling me to get Etty to bite of the *pitom* (top of the etrog fruit) of my *esrog* (yellow citrus fruit, which Jews use over the holiday of Sukkot), and this one telling me where to have kavona in *teffilah* (prayer).

We used to listen to all these ideas, but nothing helps, and every time someone tells us something, it makes us feel very upset and down. Nowadays we just say, "Thank you very much," and forget about the incident.

Unless someone is close to the person, or he's a competent rabbi (he still has to be close to the person), or if he is a medical expert in the field, they shouldn't be giving people all the stupid advice that they have heard. It really doesn't make anyone feel better and doesn't work either.

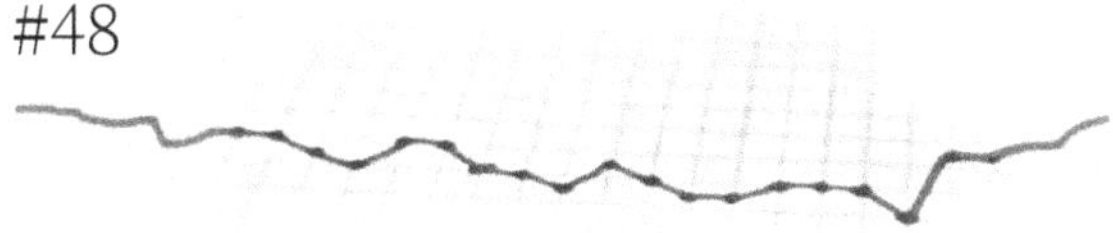

48

Happiness mixed with sadness

Today the friend Etty has been talking to about our infertility called Etty and told her she's pregnant. We are both really happy for her and elated that she can stop with all the medical things she has been doing.

But on the other hand, Etty said, "I don't feel comfortable to talk to her anymore. Imagine I tell her how jealous I am of people with babies, and she will feel awkward because she's pregnant." I don't blame Etty, and I'm happy her friend is finally pregnant, but it is a shame that Etty has lost someone to talk to.

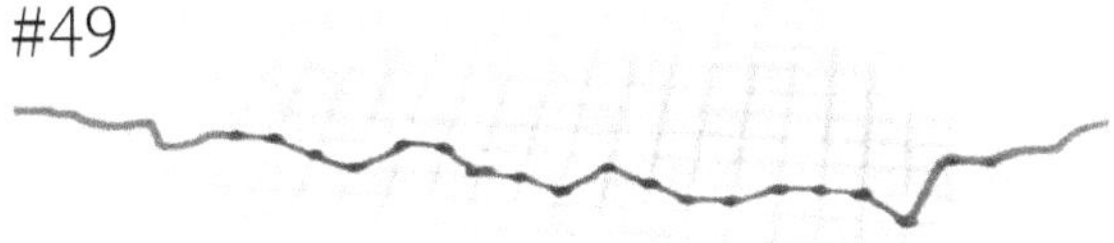

49

Back in Israel, hoping to do IVF soon

We got back to Israel a few days ago. Etty still hasn't received her period and is expecting it any day now. We have really high hopes we can go to the hospital on day two of Etty's period soon after we have arrived in Israel and start the IVF procedure.

I decided to call up my health insurance today, just to make sure everything is in order. I was shocked to discover that they didn't have anything on the system about us doing IVF, and they informed me that we don't have any permission to do it. They told me to resubmit our request.

We are devastated. I don't think I have been in such a bad mood for a long time now. Why do we need to wait longer? Why is the permission not there? What happens if we need to start everything all over again? Last time it was so complicated to get the permission. What happens if this time they make trouble again? We even have all the medication sitting in our fridge waiting!

I contacted Mrs. Melber today and asked her what to do. She said, "I will do some phone calls and arrange for you to get the permission today, then hopefully when Etty receives her period, you can do IVF immediately."

A few hours ago, Mrs. Melber told me that she had spoken to someone, and they had arranged for us to get the relevant permission. We are extremely happy and relieved, and things are looking good. Hopefully, we can start doing IVF in the next few days.

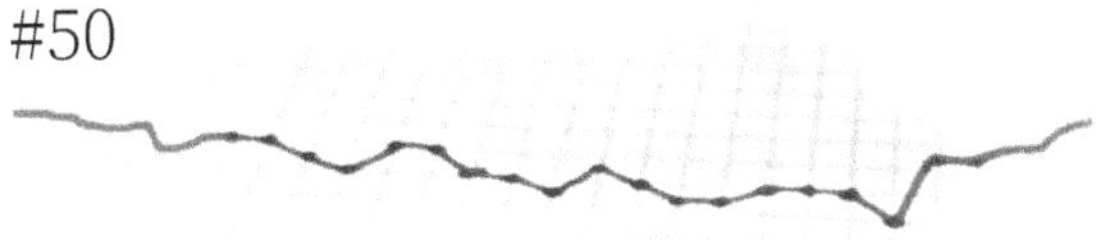

50

Hopes shattered once again

I checked yesterday to see if we have received the permission to do IVF, but after speaking to my insurance provider, they said that nothing is on the system, and we need to resubmit the request. I contacted Mrs. Melber again, and she was surprised why it wasn't there, saying she will see what she can do about it.

To top it all off, Etty got her period two days ago, which was two days earlier than I had expected. Now we cannot start the IVF treatment this month. I really thought we wouldn't have to wait any longer and we would be able to do IVF as soon as we got back to Israel.

We feel like Hashem is playing games with us. Setting us up for success, and then just before, pulling it all away so harshly from us. I still don't know what we have done wrong to deserve all this or if we have even done anything wrong at all. I don't understand God's ways, but I do know He's there. I just wish I could understand what's going on behind the scenes.

We have now been married for over three years, and we don't know how long it's going to take to have children, but we really hope it happens sooner rather than later.

51

We have permission again

I just checked online to see if we have the permission to do IVF yet, as Etty is due to get her period in the next week or so. Thankfully, it is on there, and now we are ready to start IVF. After many emails and phone calls, I managed to reapply for permission, and thankfully, it has finally been approved. We are both really excited to do IVF, and we are not really that nervous. We are happy to finally be over with our situation, and hopefully Etty will soon be pregnant.

#52

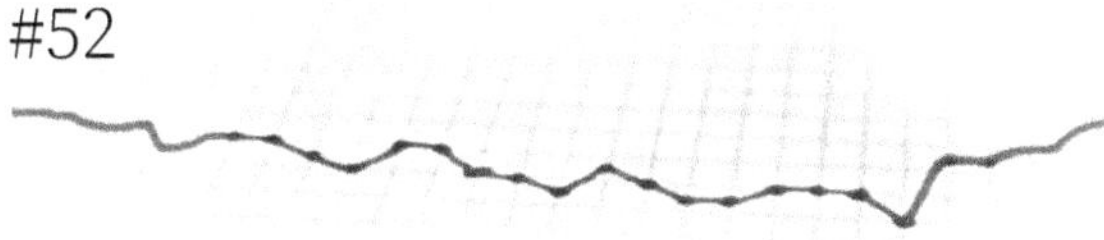

Starting IVF

Today Etty got her period. I called up the hospital and told them we will be coming in in two days' time. We are really excited for this all to be finally over.

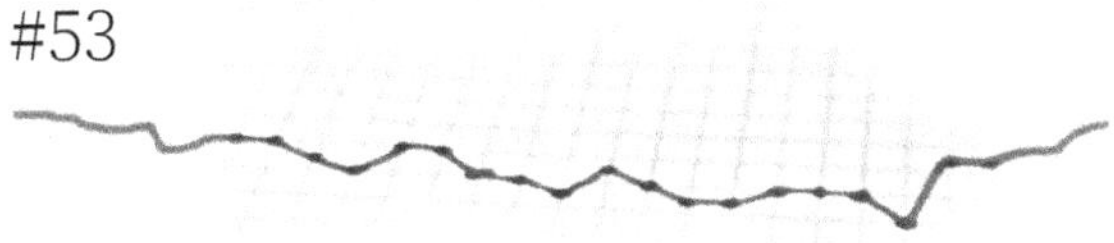

53

Hospital

We went to Haddassah Ein Kerem this morning. We got there at seven a.m., and Etty was second on the waiting list to have an ultrasound scan. After the scan, we went to nurse, and she told us everything looks fine and we should be able to start with the injection medication tonight. She once again went over everything Etty has to take, and I made sure we have all the correct medication. We then went upstairs, and Etty had a blood test.

This afternoon, the nurse called and said everything was fine, and Etty should start with the medication. She told us to come back in four days. Finally, things are starting to look good.

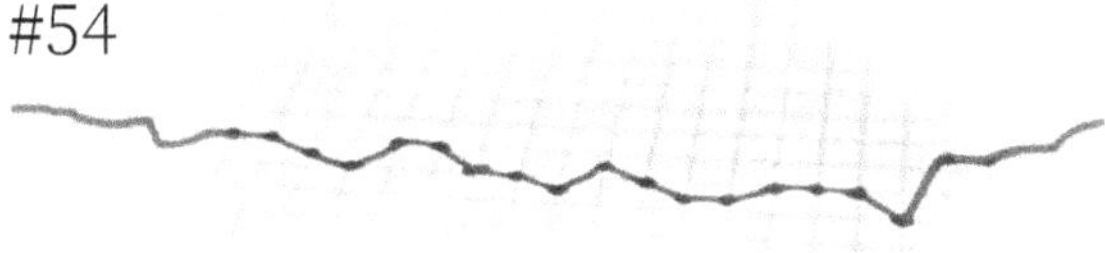

Cetrotide

This morning, we went back to the hospital, and Etty had another internal ultrasound scan and blood test. The nurse said everything looks good, and Etty should start taking the Cetrotide injection as well as the medication that increases the amount of eggs. Cetrotide stops Etty's ovulation, so that the eggs can continue growing and multiplying. She told us to come back to the hospital in three days.

I hate watching Etty inject herself, especially with the Cetrotide, as it has a really long needle. The Cetrotide comes as two parts. There is a small vial with powder in it and a syringe with liquid in it. Just before the injection, they need to be mixed together. My job is to mix the Cetrotide powder with the liquid and fill up the syringe with the right amount. Then Etty injects it into herself just below her navel. Hopefully we will be finished with all of this really soon.

#55

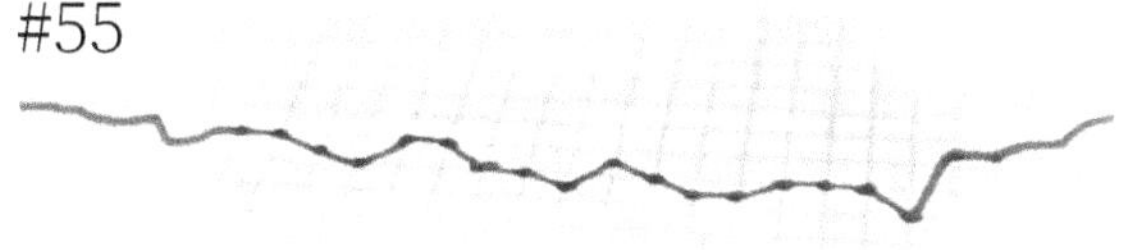

An unexpected development

Today was really hectic. We went to the hospital for the regular checkups, and the nurse said Etty was ready for the IVF egg retrieval earlier than expected. Her eggs are already big enough, and she has sixteen there. The problem is Etty is only going to the mikvah on Tuesday night, and in order to get my sperm, we need to sleep together with a condom. But we cannot be together if Etty has not yet gone to the mikvah. I was feeling really stressed and didn't know what to do. To top it all off, Dr. Dior will only be available on Tuesday morning to do the procedure, and if we do it on Wednesday, it will be done by a doctor we don't have any previous experience with.

I really didn't know what to do. How can we do the procedure if there is no way for me to get my sperm? My mind was traveling extremely fast and had already come to the conclusion that we may have to stop with the IVF treatment and wait another month. I called my rabbi and asked him if there is anything, I can do about getting the sperm. He answered, "This question is beyond me, and I really don't know what to say to you. But call up rabbi so and so, who is the King Kong of rabbi's in regard to infertility and martial questions. Hopefully, he will be able to help you." I took the rabbi's number and got through to his wife. She told me she will ask him the question and get back to me as soon as possible.

I was standing in the hospital corridor, pacing up and down, feeling really nervous that this whole month would be a waste. I must have looked like a right old idiot.

After what felt like hours, she called me back and told me that her husband had said in this scenario it is okay for me to ejaculate straight into the cup, and I don't need any condom. I was so relieved and happy that we would be able to continue with the treatment and we wouldn't have to wait another month. I went back to the nurses and told them it was fine, and Etty can have the procedure done on Tuesday.

They told us on Tuesday morning we would have to come to the second floor of the hospital at eight a.m. with my sperm, and Etty has to be fasting from midnight on Monday. They also told Etty to take the Ovitrelle injection and two injections called Decapeptyl at exactly eleven tonight; they need to really be timed right. These injections will get the eggs ready to ovulate on Tuesday morning, making it possible for them to be removed during the procedure.

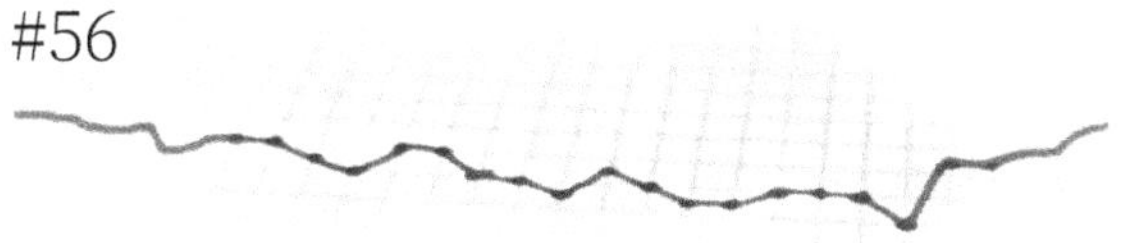

56

Friends having second children already

It's getting really hard for me. Today my fifth friend has had their second baby. Whenever I hear someone my age having a second baby, I get really upset. I kindly go over to them and wish them *mazel tov* (congratulations), I'm so happy for you. But I don't really feel happy; on the contrary I'm actually really upset. How is it that they don't have any problems having children? Why can't I have at least one by now?

57

The procedure

I'm sitting here in hospital next to Etty, and its eight a.m. Etty is wearing the standard blue hospital robe and sitting on her hospital bed. I have given my sperm in, and they labeled it all correctly, double and triple checking that our ID numbers are clearly written. We arrived at seven thirty a.m., and a nurse showed us to our ward. There are four beds here, and each bed has someone else's name written on it. Now we are waiting to be called down to the operating room.

Etty has gone in to have the procedure done. She will be put to sleep using anesthetic; the whole thing is only meant to take twenty minutes. Dr. Dior said that everything looks good, and he expects to retrieve eleven eggs, which will then hopefully be fertilized with my sperm. He said usually around eight of them should become embryos. I have been saying *tehillim* (psalms) for the past ten minutes, and then I decided to write my own prayer to Hashem: "Hashem, my father and master in heaven. One thing I ask from You, please: never leave our sides, and always hold our hands. Because Your comfort and security we all desperately need." I found writing this prayer really powerful, and I really have high hopes.

#58

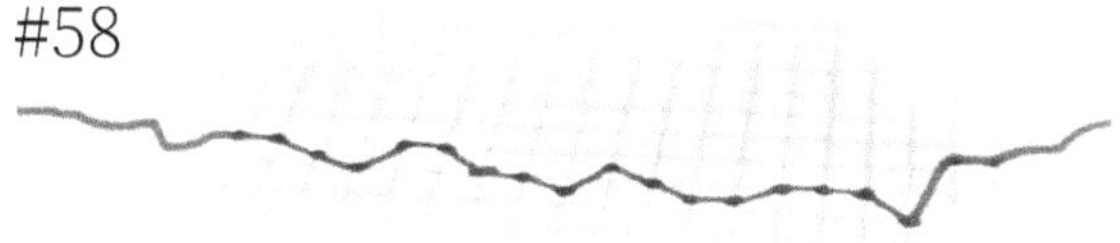

What went wrong?

I don't know what to think now. Dr. Dior just called me out of the waiting room. He said that Etty is fine, and she will be awake in the next five or ten minutes. But after retrieving all the follicles, eleven in total, only four of them actually had eggs in them. So instead of having eleven eggs to fertilize, we now only have four. He did tell me not to worry, as four still have great chances. He also said that he has just been called to do an urgent operation, so he won't be able to tell Etty the bad news, and I will have to be the one to tell her. I really hope she will be okay with it. But I suppose there is still lots of hope.

I have just spent the last ten minutes online, looking up what it means to have an empty follicle. It says that it is extremely rare, and only two percent of the world have it. It means that even though a woman can be ovulating normally and everything looks fine on an ultrasound scan, but in reality there is no egg inside the follicle, so there is nothing for the sperm to fertilize. They can only discover this when doing IVF, when they can see the follicles under a microscope. It is called EFS (empty follicle syndrome). Maybe this is why Etty hasn't become pregnant yet for the past three years. She could be ovulating correctly, and all her hormones are correct, but there is nothing for my sperm to fertilize.

I don't know what to think. I am feeling really scared and worried. I really hope those four eggs get fertilized, because who knows how many eggs Etty actually has? Maybe the rest of her follicles are empty. I have messaged Mrs. Melber and told her about this new update. She is very surprised but has told me that four still has great chances.

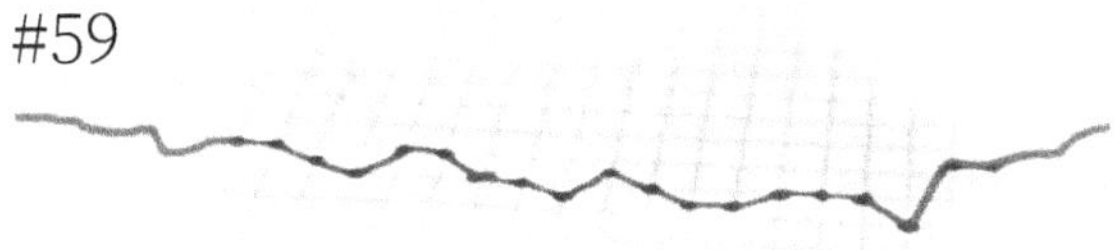

59

Breaking the news

I just told Etty what Dr. Dior said. She is really upset and is crying. I don't know what to say to comfort her. She now thinks that maybe she's broken and it's all her fault that she hasn't got pregnant yet. I said, "Don't worry, Etty. Number one, it's not your fault; you didn't do anything wrong. Number two, you have four eggs sitting in the lab being fertilized, and they will be able to use those embryos to get you pregnant." She's slowly calming down, and we are now waiting for a doctor to come and discharge us from the hospital, so we can go home. We have been here six hours already.

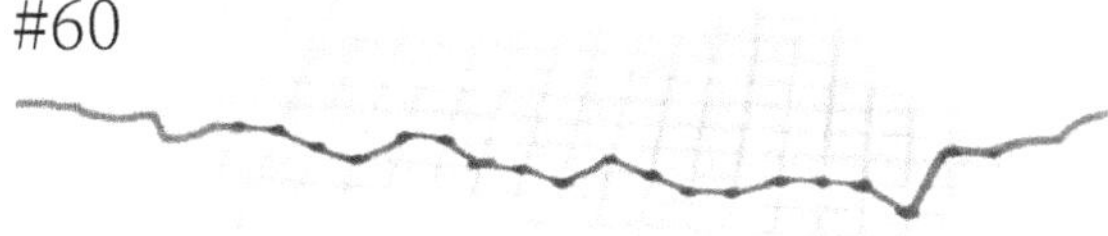

60

Failure

I just got a phone call from Dr. Dior. He said that unfortunately, all of the eggs failed, and there is nothing to transfer into Etty's uterus tomorrow. He said he's really sorry and really wasn't expecting this to happen, but we should book an appointment to come and see him in a few weeks, and he can decide a new path for us to take. I asked him if Etty has EFS, but he said they only diagnose that after failing IVF twice. He said it is also possible that maybe Etty reacted badly to the medication and that was why the follicles were empty, but both these possibilities are extremely rare. He ended the call by telling Etty to take an AMH blood test. The test can determine how many eggs Etty actually has inside her, and we should come to the appointment with the results.

I don't know what to think now. Etty is crying; I feel completely lost. What happens if we can never have children? We both so desperately want kids. Why is this happening to us? How could the doctors not have known about this? I don't really feel like doing anything now and can't be bothered getting on with my life. I know I have to carry on, especially that I need to be strong for Etty. But I can't seem to focus on anything, and I feel like my world is crumbling all around me.

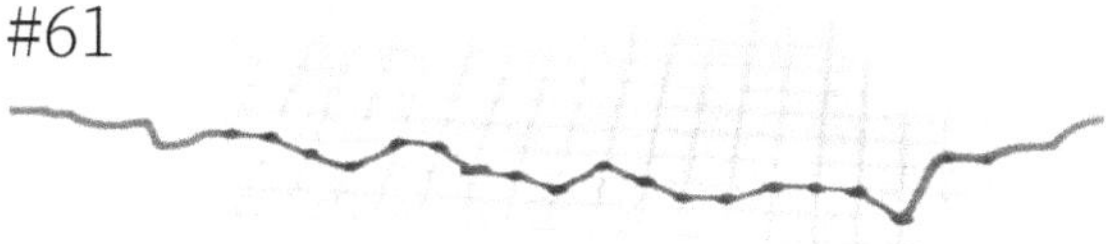

61

The AMH test

This morning, we went to take the AMH test privately. On the way back, I took Etty shopping, and she had some retail therapy, she bought two dresses, and it took her mind off her feelings for a while.

But two hours later, we received the results. The result is Etty has a low fertility number of 1. She is as fertile as a forty-three-year-old woman. Etty is twenty-one, she is young and full of life, but she has the same chance as a forty-three-year-old woman to become pregnant. I sent the results to Mrs. Melber, and she is shocked. It's extremely rare for someone so young to have such low fertility. Mrs. Melber said, "Dr. Dior will now probably change your diagnosis from unexplained infertility to this. But don't worry. I have dealt with people with a lower fertility number, and they have had children."

We are at a loss. How can Etty be so infertile? What are we meant to do now? I am feeling extremely down. I'm scared, I'm unsure of what the future holds, and I'm feeling very vulnerable now.

On a positive note, now they will be able to give a tailor-made treatment to Etty to fix the problem, as opposed to the general infertility medication they have been giving until now, for our unexplained infertility.

But I really don't know what to think. My head is completely in the clouds, and I'm extremely preoccupied. So much so that I'm forgetting things. I walk into my room to do something, but I can't remember what I have to do. I pick up my phone to call someone, but I can't remember who I wanted to call. This has never happened to me, and I'm watching my world crumbling before me. Will we ever have children? Does this mean we can never have children naturally? Will IVF work? What happens next?

Etty told me "I'm broken, and I'm sorry that you married me. It's my fault that I haven't become pregnant yet."

I said back, "Don't be stupid. I love you, and you are the best wife ever. It's not your fault that you're not pregnant. You didn't do anything wrong! No matter what happens, I will never regret the fact that I married you, and I'm sure everything will be okay in the end."

Now we need to wait for the appointment with Dr. Dior in three weeks' time, and I need to keep it together and be strong for Etty.

Afterword

I can imagine many of you are thinking, "Why did he stop the story here? What happened in the end?"

The reason I stopped here is simply because this is where we are up to in our story, and I don't know how the story ends. Although I do have faith that it will end extremely positively, and we will have children!

If you're wondering why I didn't wait a while more before releasing my diary, the answer is simple: I am so appalled about how people speak about infertility and so shocked at how people react to others experiencing infertility, I really don't think this book can wait any longer!

Once again, the whole idea of this book is only to give a small taste to those who have thankfully never experienced any form of infertility and to help them realize what we are actually going through.

The book is also for someone currently experiencing infertility, but only as something to read so that you can know what to expect. I really don't mean to make your situation look bad.

I'm also thinking that after reading this book, you might be extremely apprehensive when speaking to someone you know with fertility problems, but it shouldn't mean you should ignore them and not discuss life with them. Rather, talk to them, be kind and caring, and remember that they need someone to talk to.

Parents who have children experiencing fertility issues, please don't try to fix your children's problems. I think it is a natural thing to want to try to fix all your children's problems, but it is not always possible, especially with infertility. Be there for your children, ask them how they are feeling, let them release their emotions to you, and understand them. But don't tell them what to do or what not to do. You need to come to the realization that telling them what to do will not help them, and you need to also realize that you cannot fix everything. You are also not expected to fix everything that goes wrong.

In general, I think if you are close to someone, you should broach the subject with them and ask them how they are feeling. But I don't think you should offer them any advice. Be the person they can talk to and release all their emotions to. Listen to them, be interested, ask them questions about it, and validate their fears. Many times, you will not know from their outward appearance what they are feeling. I know myself, I put on a very good show, and if someone would see me or talk to me, they wouldn't know anything is wrong, even though my entire world may be falling apart from within.

That's why I think it's important for you to be the one to broach the subject and try to be a listening ear for them.

For those of you who have read my diary and are also experiencing infertility yourself, firstly, please realize that every single one of us has our own journey and struggles. No two people feel the same way, and no two people will have *exactly* the same problems.

But I think the most important thing for anyone going through infertility is to have someone to talk to. It's best if you have someone who has gone through a similar thing to you. But if that's not possible, then find someone you feel comfortable sharing your feelings, questions, and thoughts with. Parents and spouses are lovely to talk to, but they don't count as someone else not emotionally involved.

I also want to let you know that, yes, infertility can cause a tremendous amount of strain on one's marriage. Especially when the periods come, and when the woman is on hormone medication. But I have found that the whole experience has had an overall benefit of strengthening our marriage. We understand each other better, and we have formed a bond that I'm not sure is possible if we would have had children straight after getting married.

I also want to tell you that although I question why Hashem has been doing all this to us, in a way it has given me a brand-new outlook and brought me closer to Him. I have definitely realized that He is completely in charge, and nothing else is at play in this world. I think it is God talking to me, but I don't understand what He is trying to tell me. I have also strengthened my *emunah* (belief in God), because every time something happens that I don't like,

I say, "Why, Hashem, why did You do this to me again?" I look at it is a sort of negative strengthening, but it is nevertheless strengthening my belief in Him.

I have also come to the realization that my life where we currently are would have taken a very different path, had Etty become pregnant immediately. We would not have stayed in Israel so long, and we wouldn't have taken the path we are currently on. I have also immensely developed as a better, more caring and understanding human being than I ever could have imagined.

So no, I am not happy that we have fertility issues, but I am extremely happy how my life turned out, and looking back, I would not have wanted to be the person that my life was set to create, without any of the challenges we have had.

Lastly, I think the only thing that keeps us going is being positive. Even though it means getting upset every time Etty gets her period and hearing awful news, but if we wouldn't have that small sliver of hope, thinking maybe this time it will be different, I don't think we would be able to continue living.

So, there is nothing wrong with having down days and feeling upset, but always make sure to pick yourself up and be positive.

Good luck to all of you!

Acknowledgments

Firstly, I would like to thank my wife, Etty, for allowing me to write this book, and for reading through it, making sure that it makes sense and is all true. I understand that it cannot have been easy to go through it and experience all the turbulent emotions once again.

I would also like to thank Hashem for everything He has done for us. Although I'm not truly happy with the predicament He has put us in, I do realize that He has never given us something that we couldn't cope with or something that has completely destroyed us. He has also always given us the correct people to speak to and helped us deal with whatever needs to be done.

A big thank-you to my parents for always being there for us, for always being available to listen to my troubles, and for always supporting and understanding us in every situation.

I have tremendous gratitude to my in-laws for financially supporting us while in Israel. Living here and getting any treatment done would not have been possible without you.

A massive thank-you goes to the Tahareinu organization and especially to Rabbi and Mrs. Melber, for being there with us and helping us so many times when we were stuck, as well as selflessly giving away countless numbers of hours just for us.

I would also like to thank my rabbi, who has and is selflessly giving us his time, being there for me to pour out my emotions, answering all my questions, and giving me his wonderful advice!

I cannot forget to thank Dr. Dior for seeing us and going above and beyond to help us, as well as all the other doctors and nurses we have been involved with.

A big thank-you also goes to the women who gave of their time to talk to Etty about her situation. You have both really made a big difference to her life!

Lastly, a massive thank-you to Joel, who helped me publish this book and made it a reality. I really couldn't have done it without all your wonderful advice and editing!

Thank you to everyone. Words will never be enough to repay your kindness!

Contact Details

Please feel free to contact me through my website if you have any questions or thoughts. I will do my best to answer you as soon as I'm able.

Website:

www.jewishinfertilityawareness.com

Follow me on Instagram:

@jewish_infertility_awareness